God and the doctor we alike adore
  When on the brink of danger, not before.
The danger past, both are alike requited;
  God is forgotten and the doctor slighted.

EURICIUS CORDUS

Frontier doctors attended their patients in every conceivable type of shelter—clapboard shacks, sod houses, dugouts and tents. When a disastrous fire destroyed much of Seattle, Washington, on June 6, 1889, Drs. Clarence A. Smith and James B. Eagleson set up a canvas-covered office to administer to the victims of the holocaust. The two pioneers were co-founders of *Northwest Medicine* which Smith edited for almost half a century. Eagleson was also one of the founder-regents of the American College of Surgery.

DOCTORS
of THE OLD WEST

A Pictorial History of
Medicine on the
Frontier

by

Robert F. Karolevitz

BONANZA BOOKS • NEW YORK

Copyright © MCMLXVII by Superior Publishing Company
Library of Congress Catalog Card Number: 67-20239
All rights reserved.
This edition is published by Bonanza Books
a division of Crown Publishers, Inc.
by arrangement with Superior Publishing Company
a b c d e f g h
Manufactured in the United States of America

ISBN: 0-517-170566

Sacred Heart Hospital, Yankton, South Dakota

The building in which the Benedictine Sisters established Sacred Heart Hospital in 1897 was originally an Indian school. By then the frontier period was generally coming to a close throughout the Old West—but the horse and buggy in the photo typified the practice of medicine as it was to continue for at least two decades.

Dedication

To my Mother and Father

Who introduced me to my first doctor,
J. E. Trierweiler, M.D.,
at Sacred Heart Hospital in
Yankton, South Dakota.

Siskiyou County Museum, Yreka, California

A Foreword

From the beginning of recorded history, men of medicine have played a prominent role in the lives of their contemporaries. From aboriginal witch doctors to the skilled specialists of a space-age civilization, the healers of the past and the present have continued a relentless battle against the ills and evils to which the human body is heir.

One of the most fascinating chapters in the annals of the Hippocratic art is the story of the men and women who brought the medical profession to America's Old West.

It is particularly significant because the 19th century was a transitional one—and on the frontier beyond the Mississippi River there existed a strange admixture of science and shamanism, of "granny medicine" and legitimate pharmacology, of trained surgeon and garrulous quack.

Somehow, though, out of the hodge-podge evolved a rich medical heritage. Adventurous, hardy young physicians heeded the call of mining camp, timber town and boomerville. They patched up scalped craniums, removed arrowheads, fought unidentified epidemics and gradually overcame the medical superstitions of their generally unschooled clientele. They built hospitals, delivered babies and helped bring stability to the raucous cowtowns and ribald railheads.

Literally thousands of doctors were involved in this continuing tale of progress in the wilderness. Each of them could have written a book about what he saw and what he accomplished. Unfortunately, most of them did not.

They were too engrossed in keeping themselves and their patients alive; they were too busy wielding scalpel and scarifier to devote much time to the quill.

As a result, their contributions have been recorded in a bits-and-pieces fashion. In the literature of the Old West, they have been overshadowed by the gunmen, the mining tycoons, the trailblazers, the Indian fighters and the builders.

The purpose of this book, then, is to give the doctor his due. Being a pictorial history, its approach is broad, and the words "frontier" and "Old West" are loosely applied. It is not a dates-and-places chronicle, but a nostalgic glance backward at the collective activities of all the saddlebag practitioners from the prairies to the Pacific.

Appropriately, the story also includes the professional allies of the doctor. Nurses, midwives, pharmacists and spur-of-the-moment volunteers labored together in the seemingly unending struggle against cholera, scrofula, "wasting fevers" and the many unfathomed diseases of the era. The picture would not be complete without reference to the pioneer hospitals—and, in a little different light, to the patent medicines, cure-alls, health caves and sanitaria which flourished during the period.

Library of Congress

(Opposite page) With saddlebags, quirt and riding boots, Dr. Henry D. Robertson epitomized the country physician of the 19th century, making his calls on horseback in California's Siskiyou County. (Above) Insignia of the Army Medical Service worn by military surgeons. (Right) Pioneer doctors vaccinated when they could, but religious beliefs and ignorance of the people often stymied them.

The task of collecting the illustrative material for this volume was enormous. First of all, doctors did not seek the limelight for their professional achievements. Secondly, the limits of early-day photography reduced the availability of indoor shots, and, thirdly, the memorabilia of frontier medicine are still in widely scattered archives, attics and albums—many unknown or inaccessible to researchists.

The sleuthing, though, was a rewarding experience for the author. The nooks and crannies of history revealed endless epics of courage, ingenuity, physical endurance and almost miraculous skill. The one great frustration is that many of these individual stories deserve book-length recognition. Some day they will all be told in appropriate fashion; in the meantime, this compendium is offered as a tribute to the pioneers of medicine who turned westward when they were needed most!

ROBERT F. KAROLEVITZ

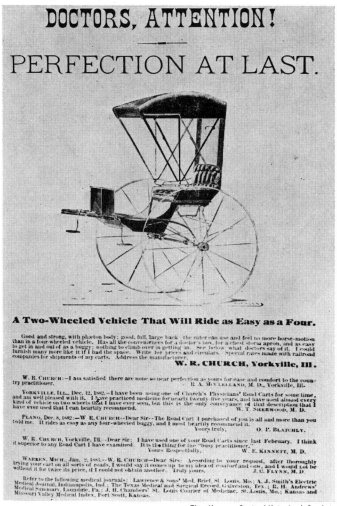

The Kansas State Historical Society

Two-wheeled carts were especially good for dodging chuck-holes, rocks and other obstacles, but country doctors found that they tipped over more readily than four-wheeled buggies. This ad appeared in *The Medical Index* in 1884.

In Columbus, Montana, Dr. William P. Smith was proud of his tiller-steered high-wheeler. Though the auto had lights, night driving was extremely hazardous, especially outside of town limits where roads were not yet ready for motor traffic. Many doctors retained a horse-and-buggy which they used for calls where cars were impractical.

Acknowledgments

Books—especially pictorial histories—are cooperative efforts. They simply wouldn't materialize if many people didn't share the photographic treasures of personal, library and historical society archives.

As a result, the author is indebted to hundreds of individuals who contributed in one way or another to this final product. It may have been an idea, a cherished family snapshot, an unknown fact or simply a note of encouragement; sometimes the latter was more important than a bundle of historical data.

It is difficult—and often "politically" unwise—to single out those who deserve special mention. It is too easy to overlook a key benefactor through an unforgivable mental lapse; yet, it is even more unforgivable not to make the best possible effort to say "thank you."

Accordingly, my first note of appreciation goes to my wife, Phyllis, who by now could well be expected to have an anti-book complex. But once again she got out more than a thousand letters, typed the final manuscript, served gallons of coffee (and a few dozen aspirin), as well as wheedling and cajoling a notorious procrastinator into action.

Many physicians helped me with technical advice and good counsel. Especially cooperative was Dr.

Herbert S. Hartley, editor of *Northwest Medicine,* who patiently answered a lay-author's questions, made books and magazines available and offered constructive criticism of considerable value. Dr. J. Roy Jones—whom I "met" only through the medium of the U.S. mail—wrote morale-boosting letters and was instrumental in providing the symbolic picture of Dr. Daniel Ream for the book's jacket.

Wherever he traveled, James W. Phillips kept eyes and ears open for medical information and illustrations, shared his extensive Old West library and acted as a sounding board during the months the book was taking shape.

Then, of course, there were the representatives of medical organizations, historical societies, libraries, universities, newspaper morgues and hospitals who responded generously to requests for assistance. At the Seattle Public Library, many staff members helped diligently with the tedious task of checking and double-checking for accuracy.

The following individuals all had a hand in the creation of this volume of medical nostalgia. To them—and others I may have left out through inadvertence—I am deeply grateful.

R.F.K.

Mrs. Stuart W. Adler, *Albuquerque, New Mexico*
Dwight Allen, *Medical Society of Sedgwick County, Kansas*
Phyllis Ball, *University of Arizona Library*
Robert D. Barr, *Lederle Laboratories*
Eugene D. Becker, *Minnesota Historical Society*
George A. Bender, *Parke, Davis & Company*
Myrtle D. Berry, *Nebraska State Historical Society*
John Bigelow, *Washington State Hospital Association*
Marie and Emmet F. Billings, *Yankton, South Dakota*
Robert O. Bissell, *Oregon Medical Association*
Don Blair, *Oklahoma State Medical Association*
John C. Brougher, *M.D., Vancouver, Washington*
Mrs. Dale Bruget, *Yankton, S.D., Press and Dakotan*
Walter F. Cannon, *Smithsonian Institution*
Edwin H. Carpenter, *Henry E. Huntington Library and Art Gallery, San Marino, California*
Ray Colby, *Alderwood Manor, Washington*
Ed Collins, *California Medical Association*
Mrs. Marguerite B. Cooley, *Arizona Department of Library and Archives*
Hugh D. Corwin, *Prairie Lore, Lawton, Oklahoma*
G. Horace Coshow, *M.D., Carpinteria, California*
Miss Virginia Daiker, *Library of Congress*
Mrs. Helen L. Davidson, *Eli Lilly and Company*
J. Calvin Davis, *M.D., Omaha, Nebraska*
James M. Day, *Texas State Library*
Miss Mary K. Dempsey, *Montana Historical Society*
Sister M. Desideria, *O.S.B., Sacred Heart Hospital, Yankton, South Dakota*
William Dochterman, *Sacramento County (Calif.) Medical Society*
Richard J. Durling, *National Library of Medicine*
Richard C. Erickson, *South Dakota State Medical Association*
Raymond F. Fagan, *Schering Corporation*
Robert E. Fitzgerald, *M.D., Vancouver, Washington*
Mrs. Alys Freeze, *Denver Public Library Western History Department*

Dr. Lawrence Frost, *Monroe, Michigan*
Leslie A. Fuller, *French Hospital, San Francisco, California*
Mrs. Howard Fulweiler, *Carnegie Library, Yankton, South Dakota*
Mrs. Natalie Funk, *Saint Joseph Hospital, Denver, Colorado*
Craig A. Gannon, *State Historical Society of North Dakota*
Thomas K. Garry, *Custer Battlefield National Monument*
Willard F. Goff, *M.D., Seattle, Washington*
Frank L. Green, *Washington State Historical Society*
Gene M. Gressley, *Western History Research Center, University of Wyoming*
James A. Hagle, *Northern Pacific Railway Company*
Jack D. Haley, *University of Oklahoma Library*
Mrs. Katherine Halverson, *Wyoming State Archives and Historical Department*
Mrs. Dora Heap, *Sharlot Hall Historical Museum of Arizona, Prescott*
Ruth E. Harlamert, *King County (Wash.) Medical Society Library*
L. R. Hegland, *Montana Medical Association*
Mrs. Ruth Herold, *Saratoga, California*
Mrs. Bernice M. Hetzner, *librarian, University of Nebraska College of Medicine*
Philip N. Hogue, *M.D., Seattle, Washington*
Evelyn Hohf, *Yankton, South Dakota*
Prof. Helen M. Huebert, *College of Nursing, University of Wyoming*
Sister M. Gladys Hunhoff, *O.S.B., Mount Marty College, Yankton, South Dakota*
Mrs. Anna M. Ibbotson, *Washington State Historical Society*
Jan and Jill Karolevitz, *Mission Hill, South Dakota*
H. C. Kluge, *picture librarian, Armed Forces Institute of Pathology*
Marshall H. Kuhn, *California Physicians' Service*
Mary Meagher, *Yellowstone National Park*
Ralph C. Moore, *M.D., Nebraska Methodist Hospital, Omaha, Nebraska*
Mrs. Lewis J. Moorman, *Oklahoma City, Oklahoma*
Myrtle Myles, *Nevada Historical Society*
William P. Neilson, *M.D., Enid, Oklahoma*

Clark W. Nelson, *archivist, Mayo Clinic*
Allan R. Ottley, *California State Library*
W. T. Parker, *Office of the Surgeon General, Department of the Army*
Dr. Hans Lee Pearce, *Portland, Oregon*
Frank Perrin, *Great Northern Railway*
Mrs. Kathleen Pierson, *State Historical Society of Colorado*
Mrs. Hazel Pollock, *Siskiyou County Museum, Yreka, California*
Mary M. Post, *Ramsey County Medical Society, St. Paul, Minnesota*
Frances E. Quebbeman, *New Salisbury, Indiana*
Roger Railton-Jones, *The Hallmark Gallery*
Mrs. Shirley Reed, *Carnegie Library, Yankton, South Dakota*
Mrs. Paul M. Rhymer, *Chicago Historical Society*
Robert W. Richmond, *Kansas State Historical Society*
Will G. Robinson, *South Dakota State Historical Society*
Robert Rosenthal, *M.D., St. Paul, Minnesota*
Edwin C. Schafer, *Union Pacific Railroad Company*
Mrs. Mildred Schulz, *Illinois State Historical Library*
Margaret D. Shepherd, *Utah State Historical Society*
Irene Simpson, *Wells Fargo Bank History Room, San Francisco*
Hollister S. Smith, *St. Louis Medical Society*
Ed Snyder, *Seattle, Washington*
Margaret J. Sparks, *Arizona Pioneers' Historical Society*
Rev. A. D. Spearman, *S.J., University of Santa Clara*
Mrs. Bertha Y. Stratford, *Seattle Historical Society*
E. R. Tarnowsky, *Harrah's Automobile Collection*
Mrs. Enid Thompson, *State Historical Society of Colorado*
John Barr Tompkins, *The Bancroft Library, University of California*
William W. Vermilye, *Seattle, Washington*
Pat Wagner, *True West Magazine*
Merle W. Wells, *Idaho Historical Society*
Mrs. Nancy B. Willey, *New York Academy of Medicine*
Guy Williams, *Seattle, Washington*

Table of Contents

Picture credits (top to bottom): (Dr. P. K. Lewis Collection) Division of Manuscripts, University of Oklahoma Library; (N. H. Rose Collection) Division of Manuscripts, University of Oklahoma Library; The Medical Society of Sedgwick County, Kansas; Minnesota Historical Society.

(Top to bottom) A class of prospective physicians posed with a well-worn cadaver; the Adolph Dreiss drugstore, a pioneer establishment in San Antonio, Texas; surgery under a gas light in the Wichita (Kansas) Hospital, circa 1900; hospitals had to overcome a widespread prejudice that they were a place where one went to die; this picture was taken in a ward of the Northwestern Hospital for Women and Children in Minneapolis.

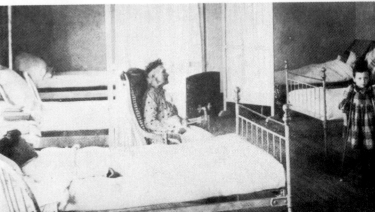

(Opposite page) Denver Public Library Western Collection
(Above) The Smithsonian Institution, Office of Anthropology

From Medicine Men to Men of Medicine

If the doctor . . . shall kill the patient or shall destroy the sight of the eye, his hand shall be cut off.

HAMMURABI

WITH permission of his tribal chief, the Apache medicine man placed the two babies back-to-back, and with a single bullet, killed both of them.

The infants were dying of smallpox anyway, and by this simple solution the medicine man was able to protect his own neck. Tribal custom permitted him to lose

(Opposite page) The Indian medicine man, with calumet and gourd, tried to banish the evil spirits which he believed were responsible for illness. (Above) A sick child received the dubious ministration of five tribal healers of the Sia Pueblo in New Mexico. The photo by M. C. Stevenson was taken before 1890. In some tribes medicine men themselves were killed if they lost too many patients.

just six patients before he himself would be done away with and by killing the two babies with one shot, he was credited with only one death.

The *Arizona Sentinel* of February 16, 1878, reported the incident almost casually in a period when two civilizations were flowing together, meshing aboriginal practices with those of a more advanced culture.

Long before the European sea rovers found their way to American shores, the medicine man or shaman reigned—albeit precariously—as a combination priest and doctor, called in to do battle with the evil spirits from whom all ills sprang. And as the western frontier opened in the 19th century, the native healer was on the scene before the first diploma-bearing physician arrived.

It is easy to generalize about the Indian medicine

The medicine bundle of the Blackfoot Indians (shown on a stick tripod) was typical of the talismans which various tribes used to placate or ward off evil spirits. Physical illness, of course, was just one of the misfortunes of life attributable to bad gods.

men, to label them all as gourd-rattling dancers and incanters who existed mostly because of the ignorance of their fellow tribesmen. In the light of later knowledge, such a conclusion may seem justified, but in the time-setting in which he practiced, the shaman was honored and respected, second only to a chieftain.

From Algonquin to Zuni, each tribe had its special middleman between earthlings and spirits. Each, in turn, had his special rituals, ministrations and healing paraphernalia—and each was governed by unwritten clan customs and laws which were often harsh and unbending.

That's why the Apache medicine man was able to murder the two babies with tribal approbation. For all the honor and glory, his was not an easy role. Others had it even tougher: lose one patient and your teeth were pounded in or your eyes plucked out. In 1868 when a whooping cough epidemic hit Indians living near Fort Mojave, Arizona, six medicine men were put

Frederic Remington's famous painting of "The Missionary and the Medicine Man" depicts graphically the merging of two civilizations. Pioneer doctors were to run into religious obstacles with both.

to death because they failed to cure their patients.

Still, there were always candidates for the job, which, with luck—and a certain amount of skill—could last indefinitely and be considerably remunerative in Indian terms.

While medicine men danced and exhorted and wielded gaudy calumets, they were armed, too, with time-tested remedies capable of legitimate cures. Without benefit of test tube or laboratory, native practitioners developed concoctions with which to treat recognizable maladies. Most of these potions were vegetable in nature, and proof of their efficacy is the fact that dozens of drugs used by Indian healers are still included in the U.S. Pharmacopeia.

Before the white man brought the curse of such ravaging diseases as smallpox, yellow fever, cholera, measles, syphilis and gonorrhea, Indians suffered most generally from respiratory and digestive ailments—and the reasons were obvious. Exposure to the elements, particularly the harsh winters, took a heavy toll. When hunting was good, the entire tribe over-ate; when rations were scarce, near-starvation was not uncommon. These gastronomical ups-and-downs had anything but salubrious effects.

And so the medicine men had their work cut out for them! From their medicine bundles they took herbs, roots, leaves, bark and berries; from these they brewed teas and tonics, or mixed myriad salves and poultices.

Pacific Northwest Indians used poultices of skunk cabbage leaves or charred honeysuckle vine in bear's

The Smithsonian Institution, Office of Anthropology

grease for bruises and sores. Washoes and Shoshones applied pitch from pinon pine and white fir for the same purpose; Paiutes used milkweed latex.

In Montana Blackfoot tribes treated kidney ailments with a decoction made from the roots of the stinging nettle; diarrhea sufferers were given sagebrush tea; cascara and sarsaparilla roots provided cathartic effect.

Omahas boiled the inner bark of the slippery elm as a tonic. Dakotas sipped willow tea for upset stomachs. Mescaleros packed arrow wounds with eagle's down. Crows ate raw liver from a freshly killed buffalo for listlessness.

In hogans, pueblos and nomadic camps, ailing Indians were treated with a primitive *materia medica*. The fruit of Oregon grape and elderberry produced an envigorating tonic; the inner bark of the latter was a strong emetic. Cherokees chewed the rhizomes of snakeroot and applied the resultant cud to snakebite. Wild tansy made a lotion for sore eyes, and smoking a mixture containing the root of devil's walking stick relieved headaches.

Native remedies were not confined entirely to the products of Nature's pharmacy. Some tribes practiced blood-letting; in central California, Indians opened the veins of the right arm for maladies of the trunk and the left arm for affected extremities. Enemas were ad-

Sweat houses were used by a number of Indian tribes to treat various illnesses. Sufferers were severely steamed, after which they plunged into a nearby stream where the shock either killed or cured. Steam was generated by pouring water over hot stones. The crude log-and-mud sweat house above was photographed near the Klamath River in 1894. Flathead Indians used an igloo-like structure as pictured below.

Oregon State Historical Society

Dr. Carlos Montezuma, who was buried near Fort McDowell in Arizona, was an Apache Indian named Wassaja. He was captured by a Pima warrior as a youngster, bought out of slavery and educated by an itinerant Italian photographer. Ultimately he became a physician, practicing in Chicago where he attracted an extensive white clientele. Concurrently, he worked diligently for the cause of Indians everywhere, and then returned to the reservation where he died of tuberculosis.

ministered, and the use of feathers to induce vomiting was widespread. Large wounds were sutured with sinew, and various types of wood and rawhide splints were used for fractures. The beneficial effects of mineral springs were widely recognized.

A much-favored device—which probably killed more than it cured—was the sweat house, a mud-plastered hut where victims of pneumonia, rheumatism and other respiratory ailments were steamed to debility and then plunged into cold water. If the weakened patient died, evil spirits got the blame.

Elderly women of the tribe often cared for the sick in the absence of the medicine man. Many of them were wise in the ways of herbal remedies, and it is possible they saved more lives than the official shamans.

Pregnancy and child-birth were generally not considered problems of medicine, in spite of the fact that mortality rates of mothers and infants were extremely

(Left) In the 1830s, artist George Catlin saw a Blackfoot Indian medicine man minister to an ailing tribesman near Fort Union. This drawing was made from a sketch he penciled from memory in 1852. (Right) Pesh-Coo, an Apache medicine man in the 1880s, had similar trappings. Skin drums, gourd rattles, eagle feathers and necklaces of everything from bear claws to human fingers were used by various tribal healers.

high. Native midwives were usually involved in the confinement rites which varied among tribes. When labor began for certain Apache women, they were tied to a tree with their arms above their heads. Nez Perces practiced vaginal manipulation. Crushed rattlesnake rattles were given orally to speed delivery.

In certain instances, abortion was considered mandatory. To achieve results, squaws jumped up and down on the abdomen of the offending women.

When the white man came with his strange new diseases, the Indian medicine man was seriously frustrated. Herb teas did not cure venereal diseases. A plaster of cattail down fried in coyote grease was ineffective against smallpox. Measles killed regardless of ministrations. Shamanism in its various forms was a last resort.

In some tribes sucking rituals were performed, with the medicine man kneading and sucking the afflicted part to drive out the supernatural evil-doers. Navajos depended upon mystic sand paintings to cure illnesses

Dr. Charles A. Eastman was a full-blooded Santee Sioux who became a college-trained physician. He returned to the reservation to minister to his fellow Indians, and was on hand to see the results of the massacre on Wounded Knee Creek in South Dakota in 1890. He described the carnage as "a severe ordeal for one who had so lately put all his faith in the Christian love and lofty ideals of the white man."

South Dakota State Historical Society

Special Collections, University of Arizona Library

Medicine men were generally highly respected among their fellow tribesmen. In addition to their incantations, dancing and often wierd rituals, they developed a *materia medica* of roots, herbs and other vegetable substances which proved effective in certain illnesses. Pictured here is Clan-na-hoot-te, an Apache tribal doctor in 1884.

attributable to the spirit world. Fetishes, charms and medicine bundles were commonplace, and ranged from eagles' claws to necklaces of human forefingers.

Then, gradually, the Great Change occurred. As the frontier rolled back, trained physicians arrived to challenge the position of the medicine man. The process was slow. Centuries of tribal custom and superstitions had to be overcome. The separation of medical care and religious exorcism was necessary if the age-old hold of the shaman was to be shaken.

Even before the final Indian war was fought, though, men like T. J. Bond (a Choctaw), Charles A. Eastman (a Santee Sioux) and Carlos Montezuma (whose Apache name was Wassaja) were graduated from medical schools. Their diplomas marked the dawn of a new era in the healing art. High noon, however, was still far in the future!

17

(Opposite page) Most of earliest physicians to reach the western wilderness accompanied exploration parties. They, of course, used their medical knowledge to treat those who fell ill or were injured on their expedition, but they also were responsible for observations and detailed notes of biological, geological, botanical and other scientific characteristics of the new country. Dr. F. V. Hayden (shown seated before his tent) explored extensively in the Black Hills and what eventually became Yellowstone National Park. (Above) Before doctors, frontier medical treatment consisted largely of whiskey, folk remedies and bowie knife probings for bullets and arrowheads.

In the Medical Vanguard

I dressed him; God cured him.

AMBROISE PARÉ

In her excellent book, *Medicine in Territorial Arizona*, Frances E. Quebbeman credits the early Spanish explorers with two dubious and indirect contributions to New World medicine and surgery: the spread of epidemic disease among the natives and introduction of gunshot wounds. In the years to come, both were to be the bane of frontier physicians.

To the Spanish, of course, also went the honor of introducing "civilized" medicine to the Old West. Three centuries before the American Civil War, medical degrees were being awarded in Lima, Peru, and Mexico City. In 1540 Francisco Vazquez de Coronado had at least one doctor to care for his 300 soldiers and the

Dr. Antoine Francois Saugrain was a French physician who came to St. Louis, Missouri, in 1800. He supplied the Lewis and Clark expedition with a barometer and thermometer he invented, as well as some experimental lucifer matches. It is believed that he was also Meriwether Lewis's medical tutor before the journey to the Pacific. This reproduction of Doctor Saugrain's workshop in the St. Louis Medical Society's Museum is complete with dried plants which the physician-chemist used for study and to concoct medicines.

thousand Indians who tagged along on the march to the Seven Cities of Cibola. Throughout the vast expanse of New Spain, doctors were treating Indians and immigrants alike—decades before the first colony was established at Jamestown in 1607.

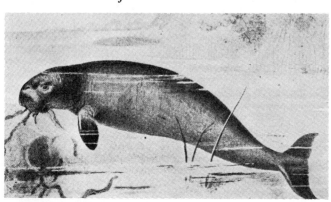

In the 17th and 18th centuries Spanish authorities extended their influence northward, in search of gold and to protect themselves against the encroachments of the British and French. A third factor was the religious conversion of the natives. Until 1767—when they were expelled by Charles III—the Jesuits were the principle missionaries. Later the Franciscan padres supplanted them. Into what is now California, Arizona, New Mexico and Texas they carried the cross—and a medicine kit.

Beginning in 1769, Father Junipero Serra led the construction of the first of 21 missions which were to

Hundreds of plants, trees, birds and animals were first seen and named by or for pioneer doctors. Dr. George Wilhelm Steller, physician and naturalist who accompanied Vitus Bering to Alaska in 1741, observed the Steller's sea cow on that expedition. The huge amphibian has since been considered extinct.

Surgery in the wilderness is depicted in this vintage sketch. Whiskey was the only anesthetic, and operations were performed by unschooled trappers, traders and adventurers. Kit Carson was said to have been a skilled hunting-knife "surgeon."

stretch along El Camino Real from San Diego to Sonoma. With and without degrees, the Franciscan friars treated ills and spread the gospel. Father Serra himself was especially interested in the medicinal value of the local flora, and he is credited with the extensive use of citrus fruits in the control of scurvy. Other missionaries scoured the countryside for indigenous drugs and surgically tackled such major cases as amputations and caesarian births.

One of the first physicians of record to practice in what is now the United States was Dr. Pedro Prat, graduate of the University of Barcelona. He was aboard the *San Carlos,* one of the two ships which brought Father Serra and the other mission-builders to San Diego Bay in 1769. Scurvy and dysentery virtually wiped out the crew of the *San Carlos,* and when the stricken passengers were helped ashore by a rescue party from the other vessel, Doctor Prat worked heroically to prevent further deaths in a makeshift aid sta-

Dr. William Fraser Tolmie, a graduate of the University of Glasgow in 1831, signed up for service with the Hudson's Bay Company the following year as surgeon and clerk. He was sent to Fort Vancouver in what is now the state of Washington to work under another physician, Dr. John McLoughlin. He was reportedly the first white man to attempt an ascent of Mt. Rainier, and his diary of early-day experiences in the Pacific Northwest are vividly descriptive of the time and territory. The old portrait, circa 1841, shows him as beardless. Artist Parker McAllister of *The Seattle Times* depicted him well-whiskered in a scene recalling difficulties he had with American squatters when he was factor at Fort Nisqually.

Dr. John McLoughlin was the "White Headed Eagle" of the Hudson's Bay Company. He became chief factor of the firm's Pacific Northwest operations in 1824, with headquarters at Fort Vancouver. In the early years, he handled both administrative and medical duties at the post, but with the arrival of Doctors William F. Tolmie and Meredith Gairdner, he was relieved of much of his practice. After outstanding contributions to the region, Doctor McLoughlin resigned in 1845 following a dispute with his superior, Governor George Simpson. He died in 1857 and is buried in Oregon City, Oregon.

tion of driftwood and canvas which is often referred to as California's first hospital.

The collapse of New Spain and recognition of Mexican independence in 1821 ushered in a quarter-century of unrest and dissension from East Texas to the Pacific Coast. Meanwhile, more and more doctors (including a few with no credentials whatsoever) arrived to practice their profession and to seek a measure of fame and fortune. They included men like Dr. James William Burroughs, who served as a contract surgeon for Mexican troops; Drs. Nicholas and Richard Den, both graduates of the University of Dublin; Dr. John Marsh, who got his license to practice in Los Angeles in 1836 with a bachelor of arts degree from Harvard; Dr. James L. Ord, a military surgeon who resigned from the army and married into a wealthy Spanish family at Santa Barbara; and Dr. Edward Turner Bale, an Englishman who came to Monterey in 1837, married the Mexican governor's niece and was promptly named surgeon general.

In Texas, missions and presidios were also being built—and again scalpels and scripture were partners in the venture. As early as 1806 children at San Antonio de Bexar were being vaccinated against the ravages of smallpox. A year before that a hospital was established in the Alamo. In 1819 an adventurous physician, Dr. James Long, led the first of two unsuccessful expeditions to free Texas from Spain. He was killed after being taken prisoner—but not until he had stirred the fires of independence which were to burst into full blaze against Mexico in 1836. The inspirational turning-point of this historic revolt occurred on March 6, 1836, when 3,000 Mexican soldiers under Santa Anna massacred 187 heroic Texans, including three doctors— Edward T. Mitchasson, Amos Pollard and Jesse G. Thompson. Four days earlier at Washington-on-the-Brazos, seven physicians were among those who signed the Texas Declaration of Independence.

Elsewhere, men of medicine were making themselves a part of the Old West's early history. In 1741

Doctor McLoughlin, who is also known as "the Father of Oregon," built his final residence at Oregon City, Oregon, where the Hudson's Bay Company had established a sawmill. The building was kept intact through the years and in 1909 was moved from its original site to the heights above the city. It was an ambitious project, as two horses with cable and capstan snaked the house up the narrow roadway to McLoughlin Park. The restored dwelling officially became a national historic site in 1941.

McLoughlin Memorial Association

Vitus Jonassen Bering, a Danish explorer in the service of the Russian tsar, landed on the coast of Alaska. With him was Dr. George Wilhelm Steller, physician and naturalist who wrote detailed reports of the area and after whom the Steller's sea cow and Steller's jay were named.

The practice of including doctors with expeditions into the wilderness became quite general. After all, they were the most scientifically trained men of their day, and to them was entrusted the mission of observing and recording the minute details of geography which might have escaped a less-qualified individual. Like Steller, some have had their names perpetuated in their discoveries. The Pacific madronna tree (*Arbutus Menziesii*) was named for Dr. Archibald Menzies, who accompanied Captain George Vancouver on his voyage to Nootka Sound in 1790. The steelhead or salmon-trout (*Salmo Gairdneri*) and the Gairdner woodpecker commemorate Dr. Meredith Gairdner, who arrived at Fort Vancouver from England in 1833.

In the meantime, Dr. John Mackay had been left ashore on Vancouver Island in 1786 to become the "first resident practicing physician" in the Pacific Northwest. He preceded, by 38 years, the arrival of Dr. John McLoughlin, the famed chief factor of the Hudson's Bay Company at Fort Vancouver. Another British doctor—William Fraser Tolmie—sailed around the Horn in the service of the same fur company, arriving at Fort Vancouver in 1833. He was the first white man to attempt to climb Mt. Rainier; later he became a chief factor for Hudson's Bay and a member of the company's board of management in Victoria, British Columbia, where he left an enviable record of service before his death in 1886.

The historic Alamo at San Antonio, Texas, played a dramatic role in the annals of western medicine. Dr. Frederico Zervan was physician in charge of a hospital established within the compound as early as 1805. Then, on the fateful March 6, 1836, three medical doctors were among the 187 massacre victims of Santa Anna's Mexican army. Though the details are unknown, it is likely that the heroic physicians practiced their profession among the wounded until they, too, were struck down.

Among the physician-scientists who explored and mapped the western frontier was Dr. Albert Charles Peale, shown at right. A graduate of the Medical School of the University of Pennsylvania, he was a long-time associate of Dr. F. V. Hayden and served with the latter as a mineralogist. The Hayden Surveys resulted in the establishment of Yellowstone National Park by signature of President U. S. Grant on March 1, 1872.

In the vanguard, too, were other medical missionaries. Foremost, of course, was Dr. Marcus Whitman, who in 1836 became the first graduate of an American medical college to cross the Rocky Mountains and the first to settle in the Oregon Territory. At Waiilatpu (near present-day Walla Walla) he and his equally heroic wife, Narcissa, established their mission, taught and befriended the Indians and served—medically, physically and spiritually—the earliest travelers on the Oregon Trail. In 1842-43 Doctor Whitman traveled on horseback to and from Washington, D.C., in a memorable trek to save the Waiilatpu Mission and to acquaint U.S. authorities with the potentials of the Pacific Northwest. Four years later the Whitmans were murdered by Cayuse Indians in a mixed-motives massacre born of hate, superstition and revenge. An

epidemic of measles among the Indians was one of the factors involved.

Dr. Elijah White—like Whitman, a combination min-

A tragic chapter in frontier medical history was the murder of the missionary-physician, Dr. Marcus Whitman, his wife, Narcissa, and 11 others by Cayuse Indians at Waiilatpu. Bitterness as the result of a measles epidemic—a "white man's disease"—led to the mass killing on November 29, 1847. Doctor Whitman himself fell under a tomahawk wielded by a chieftain named Tomahas, while he argued with another tribal leader, Tiloukaikt.

ister-physician—came to Oregon in 1837 on behalf of the Methodist Board of Missions. Later, after a falling-out with the Board, he became Indian Agent for the Oregon Territory. Traveling westward in 1842 to assume his new position, he led a wagon train of more than 100 settlers in what was the beginning of the so-called "great migration."

Still another missionary-doctor was Father Anthony Ravalli, a Jesuit who had studied medicine at the University of Padua in Italy. He came to the Pacific Northwest via Cape Horn in 1843, ultimately settling at St. Mary's Mission in western Montana where he became widely known for his medical treatment of Indians and whites alike. In 1857 he is said to have saved the life of a squaw who had attempted to hang herself. His method: mouth-to-mouth resuscitation.

There were still other doctors in the forefront of western settlement. Dr. Jacob Wyeth accompanied his brother Nathaniel on an expedition which reached southern Idaho in 1832. Much earlier—in 1807—Dr. John H. Robinson had been with Captain Zebulon Montgomery Pike on the latter's risky adventure into the Spanish Southwest. One of Colorado's loftiest mountains is named for Captain Pike—but the first white man to climb the peak was Dr. Edwin James, who accompanied Maj. Stephen H. Long's expedition along the Platte River in 1820. On Long's maps the mountain was given James' name; later John C. Fremont re-named it Pike's Peak. Doctor James made extensive botanical observations and later wrote a two-volume report about the historical trek. A score or more plants bear his name, one genus being designated *Jamesii*. Belatedly, another mountain became known as James' Peak.

Other medical men found their way into the wilderness, too, and among them was Dr. Daniel Drake. The widely recognized teacher and founder of medical schools traveled throughout much of the western wil-

Father Anthony Ravalli was known as "the grand old physician of the Bitterroot Valley." Before coming to Montana as a Jesuit missionary, Father Ravalli studied medicine at the University of Padua in Italy. A versatile man, he built the first flour mill in Montana, erected a sawmill, concocted medicines from native plants and treated whites and Indians alike. He died in 1884 from the effects of his arduous labors.

derness, observing everything and taking extensive notes. In 1850 he published the first of two massive volumes which were considered masterpieces of medico-geographic research. In later years there would be other observant, inquisitive physician-scientists—like Drs. F. V. Hayden and Albert Charles Peale—who would add to the burgeoning fund of knowledge about the Old West.

Whatever their particular mission and wherever they happened to be, the pioneer physicians applied the skills of their profession. But on the unpopulated frontier of the early 1800s, almost everyone practiced a little medicine in the continuing struggle to stay alive. Successful surgery—with whiskey and a hunting knife —has been credited to Kit Carson. Captains George

Medicine and religion went hand-in-hand with the American Indians. Even after Christian missionaries arrived and made conversions, many of the old customs still persisted. The appearance of Father John Balfe with a Blackfoot medicine bundle was somewhat incongruous.

In 1874 Lt. Col. George A. Custer led an exploratory expedition of more than a thousand men into the Black Hills. Included in his retinue were several scientists, among them Dr. J. W. Williams, chief medical officer and botanist. While the men of science took astronomical observations and gathered geological and botanical specimens, 12 companies of troopers—armed with a three-inch rifle and a trio of Gatling guns—kept an eye out for hostile Indians. W. H. Illingworth, the expedition's photographer, undoubtedly snapped this encampment scene.

Clark and Meriwether Lewis carried an extensive supply of drugs on their historic journey from St. Louis to the Pacific Ocean in 1804-05. Both studied with leading medical doctors before their departure, and their journals are filled with incidents when this knowledge was vitally needed.

As the movement westward grew in intensity, more and more physicians appeared on the trail. The discovery of gold in California hastened the establishment and growth of permanent settlements. Later, the railroads, the Homestead Act and the magnetic lure of "a new life" brought more and more pioneer families to the rough, raw frontier. As tiny towns erupted on the prairies, along the rivers and amidst mining claims, the need for additional doctors became increasingly urgent.

The era of the horse-and-buggy doctor was at hand!

One of the early problems of frontier surgeons was the extraction of arrowheads. The special purpose forceps shown at the left were invented by Dr. Joseph H. Bill, who served at various western posts. The skull below is graphic evidence of the effectiveness of primitive weapons.

Armed Forces Institute of Pathology

The Medical Record, 1876

FORCEPS FOR THE EXTRACTION OF ARROW-HEADS.

By J. H. BILL, M.D.,

SURGEON U. S. ARMY.

I HAVE devised the forceps represented in the wood-cut for the extraction of arrows, which have been made for me by Tiemann & Co.

The cut describes itself sufficiently, but I will add that for arrows not lodged in bone they should be introduced closed, and used as a snare by which the iron or flint point of the arrow may be entangled. For an arrow lodged, they are to be introduced closed, carried down alongside the flat surface of the arrow-head, opened, and then closed on the foreign body.

In length they are nine inches. From the points to the joint—which must be very strong—is two and a half inches. The handles are crossed, and provided with a ring large enough to admit three fingers. The points are one-half inch or a little less across.

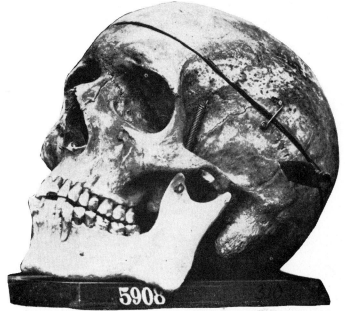

(Opposite page) **Pioneer photographer Stanley J. Morrow snapped this picture of a two-mule litter for wounded soldiers in 1876. Whether the trooper involved was actually a victim of the Battle of Slim Buttes as claimed is conjecture. Regardless, the historical photo is still valuable because it shows a medical expedient of the period. (Above) Though their pose was one of total seriousness, Surgeon John E. Bacon and his medical staff members were no doubt inwardly enjoying their photographic hi-jinks at Fort Grant, Arizona Territory.**

Saga of Scalps and Scalpels

. . . they [the medical officers] had nothing to do but to confine laundresses and treat the clap.

GEN. TASKER H. BLISS

THE role of the military surgeon in western medical history was a unique one. He was sent by the army to the scores of forts and encampments throughout the far reaches of the frontier where he ministered to the men of the command—and, more often than not, to the Indians and civilians of the area.

In his spare time he collected biological and botanical specimens, studied the local geology, planted post gardens, sent in weather reports, argued with com-

manding officers about problems of sanitation, and tried—often unsuccessfully—to cope with booze and bawdy girls, the basic reasons for many of his military patients.

On July 24, 1863, Surgeon Josiah S. Weiser of the 1st Minnesota Mounted Rangers attempted to parley with a band of hostile Sioux Indians. His murder precipitated the Battle of Big Mound. This picture of his grave near Tappen, North Dakota, was taken in 1923.

Occasionally there were unusual diversions, like the time in 1853 when Dr. Edgar Leach, the post surgeon at Fort Miller, California, provided the alcohol to pickle the right hand of the infamous Three-Fingered Jack (Manuel Garcia) and what was reputedly the head of his cohort in crime, Joaquin Murietta. The purpose, of course, was to permit the rangers who killed the bandits to collect the posted reward by delivering their gruesome souvenirs to Governor John Bigler.

Or the tragic day in 1863 when Chief Surgeon Josiah S. Weiser of the 1st Minnesota Mounted Rangers volunteered to parley with a Sioux war party in what is now Kidder County, North Dakota. In full view of the army camp, Doctor Weiser was murdered—and the bloody Battle of Big Mound began.

Or the actions of Assistant Surgeon Bernard John Dowling Irwin against the Chiricahua Apaches in 1861.

When a messenger escaped to Fort Buchanan in Arizona to report that Cochise and his braves had be-

Wounded soldiers in the Modoc Indian War of 1872-73 were transported on mule-back litters as shown in the photo on the right. An Indian-style travois was used following the Battle of Slim Buttes in 1876, according to Stanley J. Morrow, who took this vintage picture.

(Below) The Dakota Museum, University of South Dakota

(Above) (U.S. Signal Corps) Siskiyou County Historical Society, Yreka, California

seiged a detachment of the 7th Infantry, Lieutenant Irwin volunteered to lead a rescue party. In a heavy snowstorm he and his men started the two-day forced march. Their sudden and strategic appearance drove the Indians away, and Doctor Irwin proceeded to patch up the wounded. Later he joined the attack on the Apache camp and supposedly suggested the execution of six Indian prisoners in retaliation for the six soldiers killed.

The Medal of Honor was officially created by President Abraham Lincoln on July 12, 1862—and 32 years later, when he was a colonel ready for retirement, Doctor Irwin was awarded the cherished decoration retroactively for his heroism in 1861. He was, therefore, the first winner of that coveted badge of valor.

But all was not excitement and heroics!

Boredom was an almost universal curse in the long weeks and months between forays or actual campaigns. That's when the soldiers invaded the "hog ranches," as the ramshackle villages which sprang up

(Right) Many doctors who served on the western frontier "interned" on Civil War battlefields. (Below) Nineteen gunshot wounds did not stop Pvt. W. H. Brown of the 18th Iowa Volunteers, but eight years after the guerrilla attack at Cow Creek, Kansas, the Army Medical Museum case study reported his mind "somewhat impaired."

(Below) Armed Forces Institute of Pathology   (Right) Library of Congress

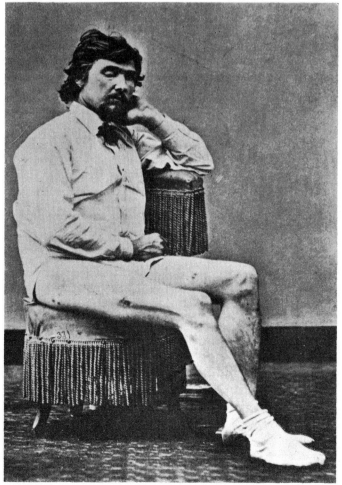

Surgeon General's Office,

ARMY MEDICAL MUSEUM.

PHOTOGRAPH No. 331.—*Recovery after the Reception of Nineteen Shot Wounds in different Parts of the Body.*

Private W. H. Brown, Co. D, 18th Iowa Volunteers, aged thirty-six, received nineteen gunshot wounds in a fight with guerrillas at Cow Creek, Kansas, October 22, 1864. 1. The ball entered the right temple and emerged under the left eye. 2. Ball entered right eye and lodged in vicinity of parotid gland. 3. Ball entered left side of neck and lodged near œsophagus. 4. Left thigh above knee—ball lodged. 5. Behind left trochanter major, *three* balls; all remain. 9. Ball entered and emerged at left axilla. 10. The ball entered two inches to the left of, and above the umbilicus, and lodged in the vicinity of the spine. 11. The ball was removed from the forehead over the right superciliary ridge. 12. Right ankle below the malleolus joint; ball extracted. 13. Flesh wound over crest of left ilium. 14. Through right great and second toes. 15. The ball entered the left shoulder and lodged in the vicinity of the scapula. 16. Flesh wound of finger of right hand. 17. Two flesh wounds of calf of right leg; one of left. 18. Right arm; fracture of radius. 19. Scratch on foot and buttock—lodged. He was left for dead. When found he had remained five days without food or drink. He was conveyed on horseback to Fort Scott, Kansas, where he remained for one year and was attended by Drs. Van Dyer and Page. Cold water applications were used. He was subsequently transferred to Leavenworth, and thence to Davenport, Iowa, and was finally discharged, July 21, 1865, and pensioned. Under date of January 13, 1868, Examiner Lucius French, of Davenport, Iowa, states that both thighs were fractured. The wounds had all healed. The pensioner walked very lame, and with much difficulty. On September 20, 1872, Mr. Brown visited the Army Medical Museum, at which time the photograph was taken. His general health was good, but the wounds were painful. His mind was reported to be somewhat impaired.

Photographed at the Army Medical Museum.

By order of the Surgeon General:

GEORGE A. OTIS,
Assistant Surgeon, U. S. Army.

31

(Above) The officers at Fort Grant, Arizona Territory, in 1886 were not outstanding examples of military bearing, if this old photo is indicative. Surgeon William Henry Corbusier, who served at numerous western posts, is shown at the left rear. (Below) The original hospital at Fort Whipple, Arizona Territory, burned in 1874. It was replaced by this building which served both military personnel and the citizens of Prescott.

near the army posts were called. Surgeons could always expect periodic "epidemics" of blind staggers, punched noses and barked knuckles. Venereal disease was an all-too-common aftermath of a "hog ranch" escapade.

When the Mexican War was proclaimed by President Polk on May 13, 1846, the Medical Department of the U. S. Army consisted of the Surgeon General, 20 surgeons and 50 assistant surgeons. Two surgeons and a dozen assistants were added in the course of the war which involved more than 100,000 American troops. Including volunteers and contract surgeons, there were probably less than 100 doctors in Mexico at any time to treat the wounded and the sick. There was such an urgent need for combat soldiers that hospitals had to be manned by patients who were able to get around enough to wait on others. The nation was fortunate that an extremely bad situation did not result in sheer catastrophe.

Assistant Surgeon William Roberts was one of the unsung heroes of the war. At Molino del Rey, he treated a wounded company commander under fire, and then voluntarily took charge of the unit until he himself was felled by an enemy bullet.

In the intervening years between the Treaty of Guadalupe Hidalgo and the Civil War, the Army had a new assignment. The victory over Mexico resulted in the acquisition of a vast western expanse two and a

Whether this ambulance was ever used as a conveyance for wounded or sick is not known, but it was typical of the vehicles used by the military of the period (circa 1876). This particular high-wheeler transported the U. S. Commissioners in the Northwest Angle boundary negotiations between the United States and Canada.

half times the size of France. There was exploring to do, Indians to put down and trailways to be protected. Military posts were erected in God-forsaken locales, and a handful of surgeons had the responsibility of keeping a widely scattered army in reasonably good health.

Military doctors accompanied the expeditions surveying the prospective transcontinental railway routes. Assistant Surgeon George Suckley served as medical officer and naturalist with General Isaac I. Stevens as the latter sought a rail route to the Pacific Northwest. Along the 35th parallel Dr. Samuel W. Woodhouse filled the same role with Captain Lorenzo Sitgreaves and his party. The doctor was bitten on the finger by a rattlesnake and finally recovered after a treatment which included whiskey, brandy, ammonia water, flaxseed poultice, blue mass, extract of collocynth, Dover's Powders, potassium iodide, tincture of iodine, peppermint water, Seidlitz Powders and magnesia cacli.

(Below) Fort Laramie, at the junction of the Laramie and Platte Rivers in what is now Wyoming, was a strategically located outpost for western travel. Its hospital, a two-story affair as indicated by the ruins shown here, was one of the largest of the military infirmaries on the frontier. (Right) A mobile pharmacy used by army medical personnel.

Farther north Captain John Mullan was building the so-called Mullan Road from Fort Benton on the Missouri to Walla Walla. Scurvy threatened the historical project, but Dr. James A. Mullan, the captain's brother, restored general health by feeding the workers vegetables, vinegar and local greenery.

During the decade before the Civil War, most of the Indian activity was in the Southwest. Assistant Surgeon Jonathan Letterman—who was to gain fame as medical director of the Army of the Potomac and later to drill what was said to be the first oil well in southern California—apprenticed in campaigns against the Apaches and Navajos. With Cochise on the rampage, surgeons like Doctor Irwin at Fort Buchanan were performing medical miracles under the most miserable field conditions. On one occasion, Irwin traveled to a stage station where a man had lain for almost a week with his left arm nearly severed by an axe blow. The wound was maggot-infested, and the doctor amputat-

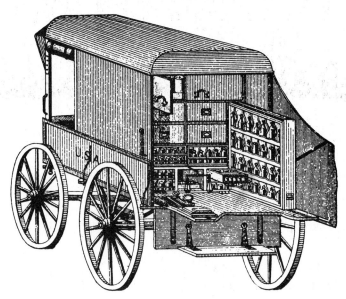

33

Dr. George M. Sternberg was surgeon general of the U. S. Army from 1893 to 1902 and has been called the "father of American bacteriology." During his western service he lost his first wife to cholera and was a hero of the Nez Perce campaign against Chief Joseph in 1877. He established the Army Medical College and served as the president of the American Medical Association.

34

Seldom has an American army unit won as much fame as the Rough Riders of the Spanish-American War. In command was Col. Leonard Wood, a graduate of Harvard Medical School who was to become army chief of staff and almost president of the United States in 1920. Doctor Wood won the Medal of Honor for his heroism in the campaign against Geronimo in the mid-1880s. Left to right in this 1898 picture were: Major George Dann, Major Brodie, General Joseph Wheeler, Chaplain Brown, Doctor Wood and Lt. Col. Theodore Roosevelt.

ed immediately on an operating table consisting of sacks of grain. The patient recovered.

When Confederate forces opened fire on Fort Sumter in Charleston harbor on April 14, 1861, the national army was a woefully inadequate force of some 15,000 officers and men scattered "from hell to breakfast" Many of the former were relics of the past, while the latter were relatively untrained and ill-equipped. Medically, conditions were even worse. About the only noteworthy improvement had been the adoption of

field ambulances in 1859; unfortunately, those which weren't broken down were being used all too often as pleasure carriages for officers.

The calamitous war, of course, brought about massive changes. Surgeon General William A. Hammond and his personal appointee, Jonathan Letterman, managed a miraculous reorganization. By 1864 (when they both left the service after a dispute between Hammond and Secretary of War Edwin M. Stanton) the Union had 204 general hospitals with 136,894 beds. A

In 1861 Assistant Surgeon Bernard John Dowling Irwin led a rescue party which routed a force of Chiricahua Apaches besieging a detachment of the 7th Infantry in Arizona Territory. Thirty-two years later then Colonel Irwin was awarded the Congressional Medal of Honor for that mission, making him, in effect, the first recipient of the decoration which was originally authorized in 1862.

Dr. Valentine T. McGillicuddy was a military surgeon, Indian agent, president of the South Dakota State School of Mines, a signatory of that state's constitution and topographer for the Jenney-Newton Survey of the Black Hills in 1875. Also accompanying the latter expedition was Calamity Jane, the flamboyant Old West character whom Doctor McGillicuddy credited with nursing talents.

total of 12,343 doctors saw service in blue—and they accomplished 29,980 recorded amputations. Two hundred and eighty six Union surgeons died during the war, 231 of disease.

Even more rapidly than it was put together, the federal army faded away after Lee's surrender. By 1866 all 204 general hospitals had been disbanded, and that year the strength of the entire Medical Department was fixed at 217 doctors. In 1870 there were exactly that many posts; consequently, the use of civilian doctors under contract became more and more common.

The surgeons at the frontier outposts experienced every imaginable kind of medical challenge. They treated rattlesnake, scorpion, gila monster and rabied

skunk bites. They amputated frozen feet and tried to relieve snowblindness. Gunshot wounds—whether by accident or on purpose—kept them probing and patching. Indian arrowheads had to be extracted. And always there was the threat of epidemic.

Doctor McGillicuddy was put in charge of the Pine Ridge Indian Agency, Dakota Territory, when it was established in 1879. He proved to be a forceful administrator, maintained peace and did considerable building during his term. When President Grover Cleveland was elected, the pioneer physician was replaced in a patronage move. Some historians feel that the massacre at Wounded Knee in 1890 would never have occurred had McGillicuddy been retained.

Another military surgeon who served in the Old West and who made outstanding contributions to the U. S. Army was **Dr. Albert J. Myer.** While serving on the frontier, he became interested in techniques of signaling, including telegraphy. As a result, in 1860, he was designated as a signal officer, the only one in the army. Later he was promoted to brigadier general and head of the newly formed Signal Corps. After the war Doctor Myer's corps took over the work of assimilating the weather observations sent in by military surgeons at the various army posts. With this basic information, the U. S. Weather Bureau was able to function as a realistic operation.

The only medical doctor to survive the fighting on the Little Big Horn, June 25, 1875, was Dr. Henry Renaldo Porter, a contract surgeon with Major Marcus Reno's battalion. In a crude field hospital—surrounded by dead horses and wounded men—the heroic physician worked ceaselessly, often under hostile fire, to save the lives of the wounded who were brought to him. After the Custer debacle, Doctor Porter practiced for a time in Bismarck, North Dakota.

Diphtheria, cholera, smallpox, malaria, yellow fever, typhoid and other diseases tested the training and physical stamina of many soldier-physicians. Causes of most afflictions could only be guessed at, and remedies were often more experimental than scientifically tested. After a serious outbreak of diphtheria ("putrid sore throat") at Fort Assiniboine, Montana, in 1885-86, the Surgeon General advised against emptying wash water and "slops" about the barracks and the use of damp or mouldy hay in bed sacks.

The military surgeons—both regular and contract—who served with the frontier commands were of varying character, temperament and ambition. A few were escapists or uniformed "bums"—and they were as bad as their counterparts in command or in the ranks. Many were young graduates seeking the excitement,

experience and travel afforded by an army commission or contract. Some Civil War veterans stayed in, hopeful of finding a gold strike or some lucrative venture in the course of their military wanderings. Included, too, were dedicated career officers who were devoted to the duty they chose.

Doctor George M. Sternberg—who was to become Surgeon General and earn the title of "father of American bacteriology"—served in the West and lost his young wife in a cholera epidemic. Doctors William Crawford Gorgas and Walter Reed, both of whom would win fame in the war against yellow fever, were frontier surgeons. Gorgas himself survived a personal bout with the dread "yellow jack" at Fort Brown, Texas. Doctor Leonard Wood, who was to become first commander of the Rough Riders and later the

Army's chief of staff, served gallantly as an assistant surgeon in the campaign against Geronimo in 1885-86. In one brief period he rode 70 miles and walked 55 with dispatches. Twenty years afterwards he was awarded the Medal of Honor for his service on the Arizona frontier.

Assistant Surgeon Albert J. Myer, developed an interest in various forms of military communications while he was on duty in the West. His hobby became a distinct asset to the Army, and Myers was appointed signal officer—the only one in the service—just prior to the Civil War. The Signal Corps he was to head took advantage of the meteorology reports and weather observations sent in by military surgeons everywhere—and, as a result, the U. S. Weather Bureau became a practical reality.

The soldier-doctors also were responsible for submitting regular reports of sanitary and health conditions at the various outposts. Some of the hangers-on who commanded the remote installations refused to forward these reports since they were often critical of the local situation, especially in regard to alcoholic intake and the consequences of "hog ranch" romances. By 1885 the receipt of these observations was made

Custer Battlefield National Monument

(Above right) Dr. Henry R. Porter was a graduate of Georgetown University in 1872. Before his experiences at Little Big Horn, he served as a contract surgeon at Camp Grant, Arizona Territory. He also saw duty at Fort Hancock, Dakota Territory. (Below) On the tenth anniversary of the battle, Doctor Porter—in white suit (No. 8)—returned to the scene of the massacre in which he played such a dramatic role.

Dr. L. A. Frost Collection

Albert P. Salisbury Photograph

Two physicians were killed with Lt. Col. George A. Custer at the Little Big Horn in 1876. One was a former hospital steward—Dr. James M. DeWolf—who was graduated from Harvard Medical School just one day short of a year before he was killed in the ravine shown at right in the picture above. Doctor Porter later found DeWolf's body and removed his personal possessions which were sent to the slain physician's widow. (Below left) Assistant Surgeon George E. Lord was first listed as missing and then presumed killed. What happened to his body has been a controversial subject of long-standing.

Custer Battlefield National Monument

mandatory by the Army; it was one of the causes of animosity between some officers of the line and the military surgeons.

At Fort Douglas, Utah, for instance, Surgeon William H. Arthur was making late-evening rounds when he decided that a typhoid-sufferer was in urgent need of repeated stimulation. Doctor Arthur issued the night nurse—an infantry private on detached duty—a bottle of brandy and a measuring glass, instructing him to give the patient one ounce every two hours.

When the surgeon returned at dawn, the patient was dead, the bottle empty and the private in a drunken heap on the floor. Trying desperately to control himself, the doctor marched the man to the guardhouse and entered charges against him.

As soon as the commanding officer heard of the case, he released the private and sent for the doctor. He told the surgeon that he had no right of command—and that the drunken soldier was not technically guilty of negligence because "nursing sick men isn't a military duty."

Fortunately, these cases were the exception. In earlier years military surgeons were ranked slightly above drummers, and in the 18th century Prussian army, doctors were required to shave officers upon request. By the mid-1800s, though, most commanders recognized

Albert P. Salisbury Photograph

This granite slab marks the grave of Dr. James M. DeWolf in a ravine where he was slain by the Sioux at Little Big Horn. The site was within the view of Doctor Porter at his aid station on the higher ground nearby. Had the Indians persisted, they might have claimed an even higher toll by storming the field hospital—but they withdrew and permitted evacuation of the wounded of Major Reno's battalion.

Parke, Davis & Company

Dr. William Crawford Gorgas, with a degree from Bellevue Medical College in one hand and an army commission in the other, was ordered to frontier duty at Fort Clark, Texas, in the summer of 1880. Two years later he was transferred to Ft. Brown in the same state where fate started him on the road to his greatest achievement: the control of yellow fever. At Ft. Brown he visited off-limits areas where the disease was rampant. Caught doing a post-mortem on a yellow jack victim, the young surgeon was arrested. Later he was released but ordered to a quarantine sector where his study of the malady was further inspired. After recovering from an attack, Doctor Gorgas went on to fame as a sanitation officer in Havana and the Panama Canal Zone. Doctor Gorgas is pictured standing at left; Dr. Walter Reed, another hero of the war against yellow fever, is at the bedside.

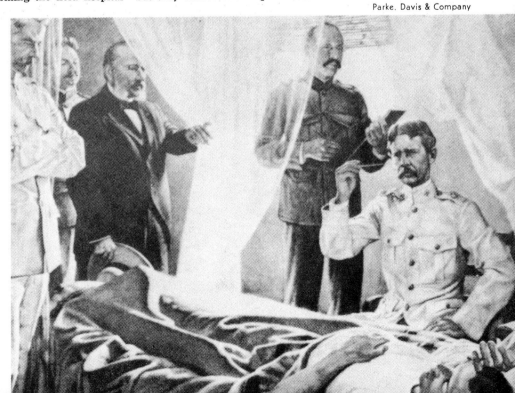

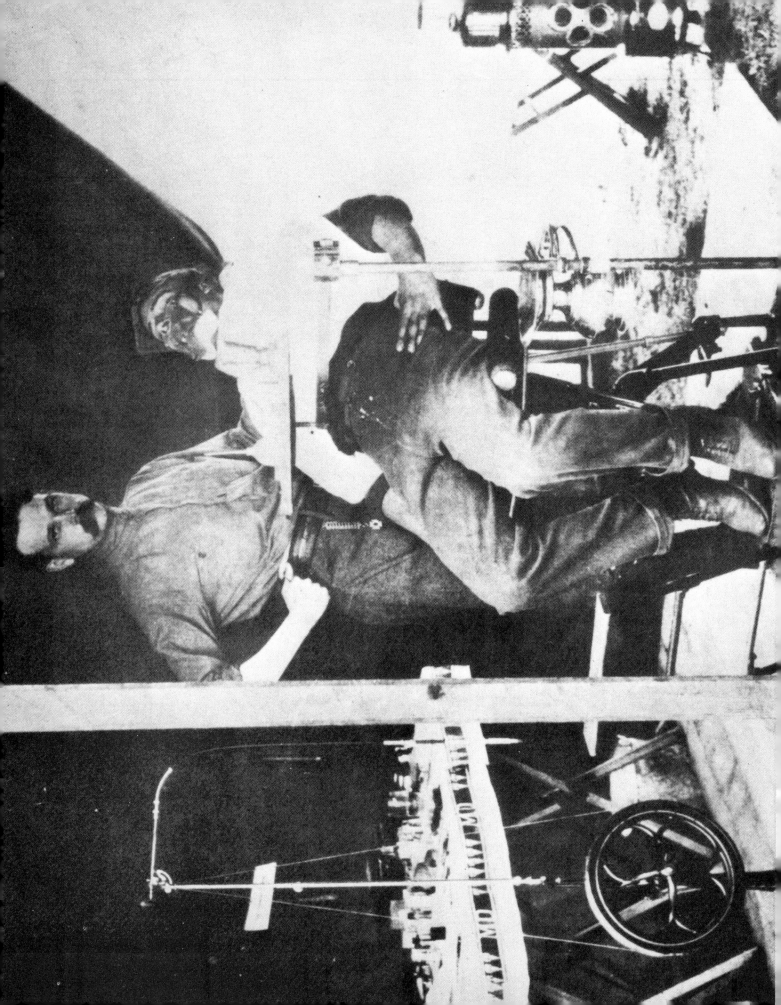

Survivors of the massacre on Wounded Knee Creek in 1890 were treated in this makeshift hospital at Pine Ridge Indian Agency, South Dakota. One physician who didn't fare well in the history was Dr. Daniel F. Royer, the Indian agent at the time of the bloody carnage. Woefully inexperienced, he was nicknamed by the Sioux Young-Man-Afraid-of-Indians. He lost control on the reservation, and his political plum became a bitter lemon.

the importance of the soldier-physicians and maintained good relationships with them. Certainly General O. O. Howard appreciated the presence of Doctor Sternberg in the campaign against Chief Joseph and the Nez Perce in 1877. During a battle on the Clearwater River in Idaho, the young surgeon heroically treated the wounded under fire and then kept 25 of them alive on a rugged cross-country trek to Grangeville some two dozen miles away.

A year earlier Dr. Henry R. Porter, a contract surgeon with Major Marcus A. Reno's battalion at the Little Big Horn, labored for 40 hours in a crude field hospital—amputating, suturing and dressing the wounds of more than 50 troopers who had felt the cold steel and hot lead of the wrathful Sioux. Two other doctors—Assistant Surgeon George E. Lord and Acting Assistant Surgeon James M. DeWolf—met death with Lt. Col. George A. Custer on that fateful June 25.

There were countless other stories of heroism and professional achievement during the colorful period when the military surgeon was answering the call of duty in the Old West. Not only did these soldier-medics fulfill their mission in uniform, but when they doffed the blue, many of them hung their shingles in the spanking new towns on the frontier they helped to open.

(Opposite page) Armed Forces Institute of Pathology
(Opposite page) On frontier military posts dental work—if any —was done by the medical doctor. Later contract dentists were hired when they were available. It wasn't until February 2, 1901, that the Dental Corps officially came into being. Field dentistry as shown in this photo was little practiced until late in the century.

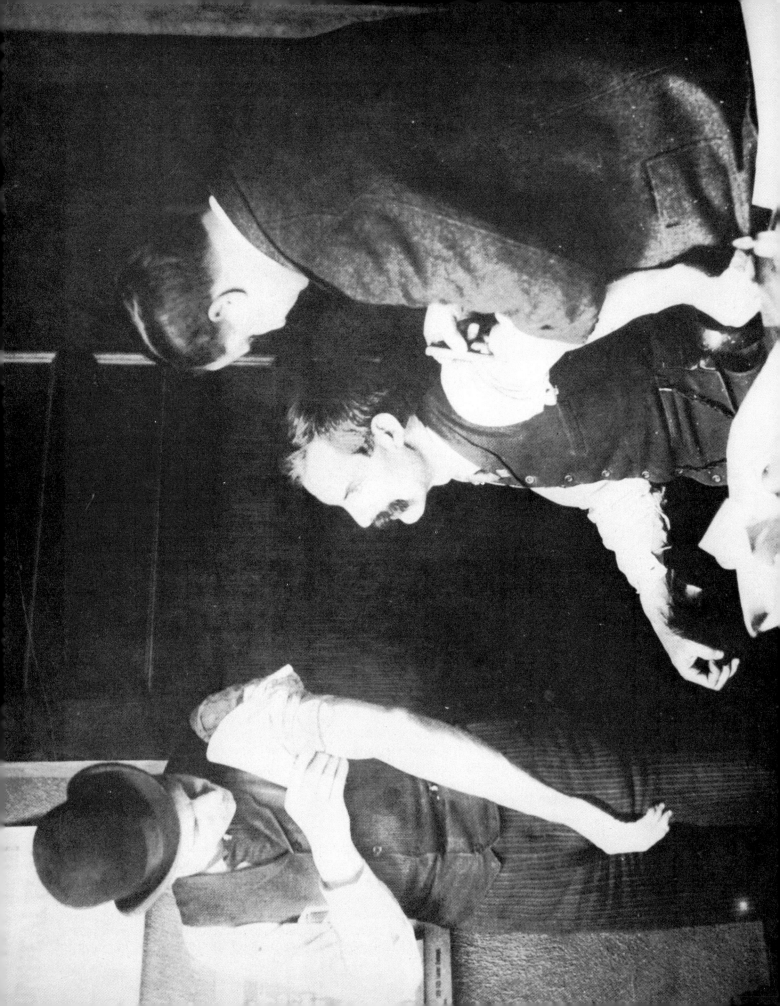

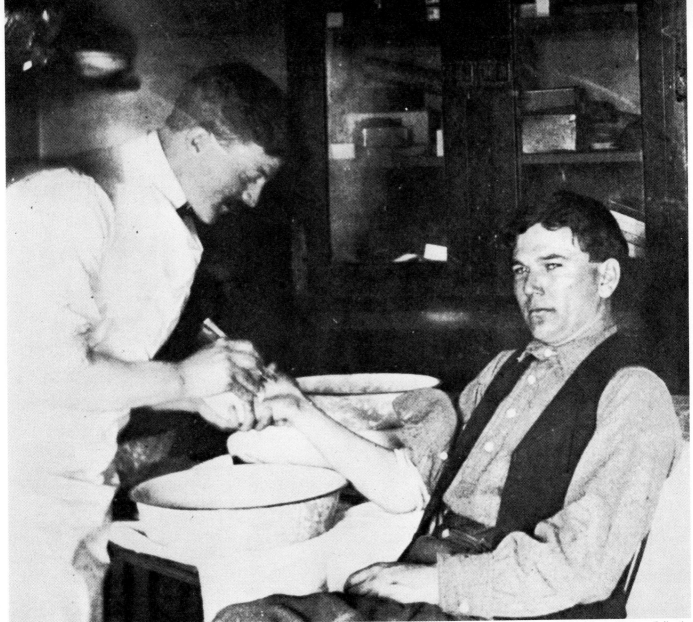

(Opposite page) Vaccinations for smallpox were administered throughout the 19th century. Vaccine and direct person-to-person techniques were both used. In the latter years of the 1800s, the bacterial cause of disease became known, so new methods and a wider use of preventive measures were adopted. The Minneapolis Board of Public Health conducted the vaccinations shown in this photo. (Above) A cowboy had his hand treated by a country doctor in Cambria, Wyoming.

Purge, Blister and Bleed

I'm delivering babies to babies that haven't been paid for yet!

SAMUEL GORDON BROOKS, M.D.
Anacortes, Washington

THE story goes that when Dr. Henry Bergsteine first arrived at Pioche, Nevada, in 1872, he went directly to the town cemetery. There he strolled from tombstone to tombstone to find out what the local residents were dying from—and what diseases he'd most likely have to treat. Pioche lore insists that of the 108 graves the young doctor found, only three of the occupants had died of natural causes!

The wife of Dr. Fayette Clappe, pioneer practitioner on the Feather River in California, confided to her diary that in less than a month "we have had several murders, many fearful accidents, bloody deaths, whippings, a hanging, an attempt at suicide and a fatal duel."

In boisterous Deadwood, doctors who treated the victims of stabbings, shootings and assorted misfortunes in the saloons and bawdy houses along the in-

smallpox and measles struck down young and old alike.

The doctors who volunteered to enter this medical battleground cannot be described in one broad generalization. Mostly, though, they were adventuresome, wealth-seeking young men from "back East" or from Europe. Their medical degree—if they had one—was their passport to a life of excitement in a new land. They could practice if they wished—or they could pan for gold or file a claim. Some traveled westward—especially to Arizona and New Mexico—for their own health, to try to overcome the dread scrofula attacking their lungs in some strange way they were unable to fathom.

There were, of course, the military surgeons who finished tours of duty at western outposts and then remained as private practitioners. There were railroad

Dr. L. Rodney Pococke was apparently the first physician to establish himself in Helena, Montana, in 1863. Like other early practitioners he came both for gold and for his health. He found neither. Within two years he was dead of "consumption."

Dr. Warren E. Day, who came to Arizona Territory first as a contract surgeon at Fort Verde, was typical of frontier doctors in some ways and in some ways not. He built hospitals, engaged in mining and ranching ventures and was politically active. In Prescott he wore a plug hat and carried a silver-headed cane, and in his later years was said to have "the geniality of an aged orangutan, being deprived of an orange." He spent a year in prison for bigamy.

famous Line also carried a stomach pump to disgorge the poisons swallowed by miscreant lasses who were continually trying "to end it all."

Needless to say, if the Old West offered a fertile field of endeavor for any profession, medicine was it. It was a land of vigor and violence, where great physical exertion was commonplace and where even the slightest rebuff could erupt into a deadly showdown with six-shooter or stiletto. It was a vast rugged expanse where drought, malnutrition and exposure to the harsh elements took a heavy toll. Though beautiful and rich and productive, it was a land of devastating epidemics, where wasting fevers and respiratory diseases were rampant, while such killers as cholera,

(Opposite page) This is what the dapper doctors of Denver wore in 1873. Six physicians were among this group of dandies posing before a local drugstore where they undoubtedly had prescriptions filled.

French Hospital, San Francisco, California

Two clean-shaven faces were among the new intern-residents at the French Hospital, San Francisco, in 1895. It might have been a matter of gradually changing styles—but more than one woman doctor was advocating the doing away with beards and mustaches as a sanitary measure in surgery.

surgeons, medical missionaries and Indian agency physicians. Included, too, were a few wife-deserters and men with tainted backgrounds who hoped for a new start on the frontier where no one questioned a stranger's past.

Generally, all of them came to be known as horse-and-buggy doctors, and a romantic aura of indefatigability, selflessness and courage grew up around them. But just to keep the record straight, there were a few who didn't fit the mold. With their medical degrees proudly emblazoned on the wall, there were those who foisted upon ignorant patients the most objectionable forms of quackery. Others—largely because of drudgery and near-exhaustion—reached too often into their saddlebags for "a little help" from the whiskey, opium or morphine they always carried. History also records an occasional coward who ran from the scene of an epidemic, and a tiny handful of greed-stricken individuals who offered far, far less than their profession expected of them.

All the rest—the vast majority—were honorable, hard-working medical servants who overcame the reputations of the blacksheep among them and made the title of Country Doctor one of which they could be justifiably proud!

Theirs was not a glamourous role, and often the monetary rewards were meager indeed. Bills were frequently paid in such "legal tender" as cord wood, chickens, canned goods, calves and cabbages; sometimes labor was traded; on a good many occasions the doctor got nothing at all.

In a letter to a fellow physician back East in 1850, Dr. Thomas M. Logan wrote about conditions in California: "I have seen M.D.'s driving ox teams . . . laboring in our streets . . . serving at bar-rooms, monte tables, boarding house, etc., and digging and delving among the rocks and stones."

Still, the pioneer physicians were generally respected individuals in the community, and often they were called upon to take a leadership role in a civic

Dr. William L. Steele has been referred to as Montana's "grand old man of medicine." He was both preceptor and college-trained in his native South Carolina. He first served as a contract surgeon in railway construction camps before opening his own office in Central City, Colorado, but when gold was discovered in Montana, he joined the throngs headed for Bannack. Though established as a physician, Doctor Steele became deeply involved in business and politics.

He operated a freight line between Virginia City and outlying camps and was elected president of the Fairweather Mining District. Later he raised horses and mules on his ranch for stage and freighting firms, profited from his own transportation company and struck it rich in a gold venture. He also became sheriff of Lewis and Clark County.

Then, in 1873, he sold out his business interests, withdrew from politics and returned to the practice of medicine where he developed a widespread reputation both for his skill and his willingness to go anywhere he was needed.

Public office ultimately lured him back, and he served as mayor of Helena, coroner, county treasurer and state legislator. He died in 1909.

In this 1897 picture, Doctor Steele posed on the steps of St. John's Hospital in Helena.

Drs. Edward Spencer, Justus Ohage and Parks Ritchie—pioneer practitioners in St. Paul, Minnesota—consulted in the Ritchie-Ohage waiting room some time during the 1890s. The nurse was Miss Ida Renne. Earlier doctors often combined all activities in a single room, with patients being examined or treated in the presence of those next in line.

project, a vigilante movement or a social soiree. Usually they had a mite more education than the townsfolk around them, and their mien tended to be less earthy than the cowboys, miners and gandy dancers they treated. Some dressed in stovepipe hats and Prince Albert coats as garb befitting their profession, but by and large, the doctors were like anyone else on the frontier—individuals with their own foibles, strengths

and personality traits. To endure, though, all required an extra measure of physical stamina, ingenuity approaching genius and a philosophy of life to bear up under professional strains and personal adversity.

While life in the Old West varied from place to place and from year to year, it was generally an existence to challenge the constitution of a martyr on the rack. Blizzards, dust storms, grasshopper plagues, Indian atrocities, earthquakes, prairie fires, fearful droughts, the terrorism of lawless brigands, flash floods and starvation were all included in the pioneer's litany of misfortune. And as if these weren't enough, there were also sickness and disease to decimate families and to add to the sorrow shared by so many eager immigrants. The winning of the West was a bittersweet victory at best; that it was "won" at all must certainly be attributed to a major miracle in human perseverance.

Up to his elbows in the accomplishment of this miracle was the country doctor!

The obstacles which faced the pioneer physician were monstrous. They included great geographical distances between patients; drugs and medicines of doubtful efficacy; a scarcity of proper equipment; a woeful lack of knowledge, and, unfortunately, the habits and habitations of the people.

No wonder people got sick when they lived in dugouts, dank sod houses, flimsy claiming shacks and crude log huts with earthen floors. Clothing was often inadequate, especially during the winter months—and diets of beans, salt pork and green coffee were debilitating, to say the least. The women tried desperately to improve the fare, but their culinary experiments with strange plants sometimes proved disastrous, and the foods they attempted to preserve were frequently tainted by the time they were eaten. Rules of sanita-

Dr. T. S. Chapman (at desk) practiced in McAlester, Oklahoma Territory, at the close of the 19th century. His office boasted an electric light, but it also included such "un-modern" items as spittoon, bowl-and-pitcher and the less-than-sanitary "slop pail." The period was one of transition, though, and in time these reminders of a septic past faded into history.

tion were little understood. Garbage was scattered promiscuously; flies which infested outdoor toilets were a continuing menace; spitting was condoned indoors and out; dead animals lay unburied until coyotes or buzzards reduced them to bones; water supplies came from seepage ditches, stagnant pools or uncovered cisterns (everybody, of course, drank from the same bucket with a tin cup or gourd dipper). The *Phoenix* (Ariz.) *Herald* in 1882 was somewhat outraged because local saloon-keepers were washing their spittoons in the same irrigation ditches used by many residents as a source of cooking and drinking water.

And so illness struck. If it got bad enough, the doctor was sent for and assigned the responsibility for the patient's recovery—against odds which no reasonably sober faro dealer would accept. To his everlasting credit, the country doctor tried hard. After a weary journey by horseback or buckboard, he would maintain a vigil beside his charge until total exhaustion forced him to a straw mattress. Strangely enough, these lengthy watches—to death or to signs of recovery—added to medical knowledge as doctors sometimes observed the full course of a particular disease, noting reactions and conditions which would be helpful on future occasions.

Meanwhile, depending upon his training—or lack thereof—the physician would administer the drugs or perform the operations he believed were required. It might be a massive dose of calomel, the favorite cathartic of the era; or a solution of tartar emetic to produce vomiting and perspiration. "Spanish fly," a drug derived from a small beetle, might be adminis-

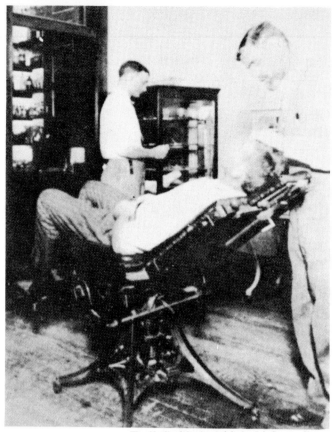

The Medical Society of Sedgwick County, Kansas

Pioneer doctors were almost entirely general practitioners—medical jacks-of-all-trades. However, by the 1890s, the concept of specialization was becoming more and more common, and men like Dr. J. G. Dorsey of Wichita, Kansas, were concentrating on work they knew best. In Doctor Dorsey's case, he was an eye specialist who developed a considerable reputation for removing cataracts and correcting crossed-eyes.

This combination waiting-and-working room in Wichita, Kansas, was not uncommon in pioneer medicine. The more bashful patients found the arrangement somewhat unnerving.

The Medical Society of Sedgwick County, Kansas

tered locally to produce a blister or counter-irritant. Blood-letting—up to 12 ounces at a time—was a common practice; or if the patient was too weak for the lancet, a live blood-sucking leech was applied to the skin. To purge, blister and bleed was an accepted treatment through much of the 19th century.

As for surgery, the frontier physician did what he could under the circumstances. Amputations—with or without anesthesia—were extremely common, partly because of the battlefield training of many of the doctors in the Civil War and partly because they didn't know of any other way to save a patient from more disastrous effects. The toes and fingers of frost-bite victims were quick to go, but hands and feet were not spared if the doctor believed that mortification had occurred. In 1889 the *New Northwest* in Deer Lodge, Montana, reported on the removal of two frozen toes by Dr. J. A. Mee. "This," the paper said, "makes twenty-two toes Dr. Mee has amputated within three months."

Tumors which a doctor could see or feel were sometimes operated for, but other internal disorders were often baffling to the physician who had neither the

FEE BILL.

Each visit by day, (6 a. m. to 10 p. m.)	$ 2 00.	**DISLOCATION:** Reduction of			
" Night visit, (10 p. m. to 6 a. m.),.........	5 00.	Finger or Toe..................	$ 5 00.		
' Consultation visit by other than attending		Wrist........................	10 00.		
physician	10 00.	Elbow	20 00.		
" Office call....................	1 00.	Head of Radius	5 00.		
" Dressing at office subsequent to first of ordi-		Shoulder.....................	10 00.		
nary injuries..............	1 00.	Clavicle.....................	15 00.		
" Administration of chloroform	5 00.	Ankle.......................	20 00.		
		Knee	20 00.		
EYE:		Hip	50 00.		
" Removing foreign body from	$2 00 to 5 00.				
" Excision of	25 00.	**AMPUTATIONS:**			
Contused Wounds, visit and first dressing,	2 00.	Finger or Toe.............	10 00.		
Lacerated and Incised Wounds, visit and		Each additional Finger or Toe...	5 00.		
first dressing, according to severity		Foot anterior to Ankle........	25 00.		
and extent......................	$3 00 to 10 00.	Leg below Knee.............	50 00.		
		Leg above Knee.............	50 00.		
FRACTURES: Reduction and first dressing of		Leg at Hip Joint............	100 00.		
Finger or Toe......................	10 00.	Arm below Elbow...........	50 00.		
Each additional Finger or Toe	3 00.	Arm above Elbow...........	50 00.		
Single bone of Fore-Arm............	10 00.	Arm at Shoulder Joint........	75 00.		
Both " " " "............	20 00.				
Involving Elbow.................	20 00.	**ARTERIES:** Ligation of (not consequent up-			
Arm above Elbow................	20 00.	on amputation)............			
Clavicle........................	10 00.	Below knee or Elbow	$3 00 to 25 00.		
All Ribs on one side............	15 00.	Between Elbow and Shoulder.	$5 00 to 25 00.		
Inferior Maxillary...............	15 00.	Subclavian..................	50 00.		
Nose...........................	5 00.	Common or either Carotid....	100 00.		
Spine, including P. P. jacket,........	25 00.	Temporal or Occipital.......	10 00.		
Tibia...........................	10 00.	Small Artery about the face....	5 00.		
Fibula..........................	10 00.	Femoral	50 00.		
Both bones of Leg..............	20 00.	Profunda	25 00.		
Thigh	25 00.	Common External or Internal			
Pelvic bones..................	20 00.	Iliac......................	100 00.		
Trephining and Elevating fracture of		External Epigastric....	25 00.		
Cranium.....................	100 00.				

Traveling long distances to be computed by time consumed and services performed.

Any services not mentioned, to be charged for upon a basis corresponding with this scale.

* Approximate Date - 1880.

Western Research Center, University of Wyoming Library

Wyoming State Archives and Historical Department

Dr. Thomas G. Maghee, who came west as a military surgeon and then remained in Wyoming as a private practitioner, made his prices explicitly clear by publishing a Fee Bill shown at left, circa 1880. While charges for medical service varied according to time and locale, Doctor Maghee's rates indicated a general level for the period.

experience nor the equipment to accomplish a proper diagnosis. In many instances, appendicitis was simply termed "knotted bowels," and surgery was not performed. When an operation was attempted, the settings were often unusual. Doctors wielded scalpels under cottonwood trees, in carpenter shops, on wagon beds, in saloons and on kitchen and billiard tables. Sometimes boiling water was available; sometimes not. Inexperienced members of the patient's family often assisted—holding lamps, chasing flies and administering chloroform with a wadded cloth. It was not unusual for these volunteer aides to faint at critical moments. One country doctor completed his first appendectomy (he'd never even *seen* one previously) at night in a farm kitchen by the light of a fire on the floor where his quaking helper had dropped a kerosene lantern.

Medical memoirs are crammed with instances of inventive genius as country doctors made spur-of-the-moment devices for particular emergencies. The bail from a lard pail was converted into a vaginal packer by an Idaho physician. Dr. John Patterson in Oregon fashioned a tiny cylindrical trephining saw out of a metal thimble and the handle of a feather duster. Another physician inserted a hollow cane pole to drain an abdominal abscess. They all worked!

And so it was that the horse-and-buggy doctor played his invaluable role on the frontier. With his saddlebags or satchel, he brought confidence and new spirit to anxious, sorrowing families. Many times he accomplished more in a humanistic way than in a scientific one. Occasionally he was condemned by the ignorant, but then, too, he sometimes got credit for what he didn't do. Over the years it all evened out.

While his weary missions were not always successful, the country doctor—with few exceptions—came to be recognized as a symbol of hope and of tireless service. He was someone the pioneer families could turn to for help when things looked the bleakest!

(Opposite page) Getting a medical education required a strong stomach in the early days when conditions for anatomical studies were obviously crude. At least these students had cadavers to dissect; many doctors received diplomas without ever seeing one. (Above) Med students always enjoyed a touch of macabre humor. Identifiable (with mustache) was Julius A. Hohf, who received his degree from Northwestern University Medical School and then practiced for many years in Yankton, South Dakota.

Regulars, Eclectics and God-Knows-What

To our mind, a graduated blockhead is more to be dreaded . . . than a self-constituted, spontaneous quack, whose advertisement betrays the nature of his claims.

JOHN F. MORSE, M.D.
California, 1856

THERE was a time in America's Old West when becoming a doctor required little more than the inclination.

No one will ever know how many men called "Doc" practiced their own version of medicine with neither degree nor formal education. At the time, they filled a gigantic void, and—to their great credit—many of them achieved a professional level which few "diploma doctors" could boast.

But, at best, it was an on-the-job learning process with success or failure measured in terms of life or death. In retrospect, it is obvious now that even the school-trained physicians were more ignorant of the

55

Posing with a cadaver seemed to be the thing to do in the medical schools of the 1890s. Actually, though, things had come a long way by that time, because students of an earlier day had to rob graves (which some of them did) or wait hopefully for a hanging in order to get a body for educational purposes. Religious opposition had much to do with this situation.

science they pursued than they could possibly have imagined.

Until the work of Louis Pasteur, Joseph Lister and Robert Koch established and then proved the bacterial theory of disease, doctors labored in a never-never land of "divided opinions." The philosophies of past centuries ran head-on into new ideas. There was ever the continuing belief by many that illness, somehow, was sent by a vengeful God as punishment for transgressions. The Four Humours of Hippocrates managed to be dragged into the 19th century. The miasmic approach—that pestilence rose from the rotted materials of earth and swamp—had numerous disciples. Galvanism, Mesmerism, Brunonism, homeopathy, eclecticism and dozens of other medical creeds and conjectures were preached and practiced.

It was little wonder that George Washington was virtually bled to death in his final illness; that tar barrels were burned in the streets of epidemic-stricken cities; that strange medicines and stranger devices came into vogue.

In varying degrees, all of these philosophies and

fantasies found their way to the western frontier, brought there by the men and women who established medical beachheads and then began to practice as they had been trained. The homeopaths administered their tiny doses; the allopaths purged their patients drastically; the hydropaths bathed and dunked; and the eclectics borrowed a little from each.

The first doctors to be trained in America were products of a medical apprentice system. Young men with a desire to practice associated themselves with older physicians for whom they swept floors, mixed medicines, curried horses and did other menial chores in a semi-servant capacity. For this they were permitted to observe, to read what medical books might be available and to learn directly all that their preceptor would and could teach them. It was a practical system, often limited more by the teacher than the student. After several years—when the doctor was convinced of his pupil's proficiency—a certificate denoting that fact was issued. Then, if the young man could afford it, he went to Europe to add to his knowledge at one of the universities. If the funds were not available, he went into practice.

Before 1800 several medical schools were organized in the United States. In 1765 the College of Philadelphia (later the University of Pennsylvania Medical School) became the first, followed three years later by King's College of New York. Then came Harvard in 1783, Dartmouth in 1798 and Transylvania University in 1799. It was a slow, but sound beginning, with the schools supplementing rather than replacing the apprentice method. All went well until the demand far exceeded the supply!

With the opening of the West, the need for doctors became increasingly critical. Each new boomertown along the railroad line wanted at least one physician. The railroads themselves required surgeons for their construction crews, just as the Army did for its frontier posts. Gold camps and timber towns were also in the market for medical aid. The result was a new approach to education.

With few laws to govern them, many established doctors recognized the opportunities for a lucrative sideline. Medical schools began to pop up like

(Above) Medical schools popped up throughout the nation when the western expansion began. Many of them were totally inferior and dropped by the wayside; others persisted and ultimately became associated with established universities. The Kansas Medical College of Topeka, for instance, became the Washburn College School of Medicine. (Below) An 1895 class at the Louisville (Ky.) Medical College "with friend."

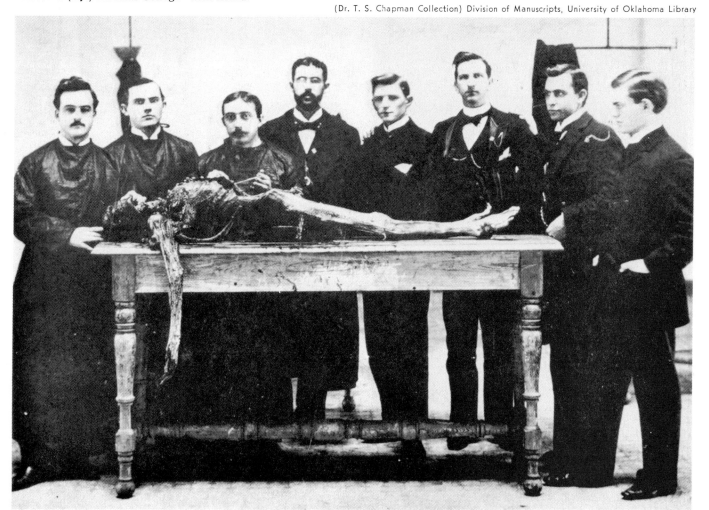

gooseflesh. Unfortunately, the greed factor often over-came the proper motives. Though some of the institutions tried to provide a high standard of instruction, others were not so inclined. Tuition fees were pocketed, a cursory lecture series on medical theory was presented and a new class of doctors was literally pushed into the street. It was a period of the "diploma mill," when inferior schools signaled the end of the limited but more practically-oriented apprentice system.

More than 400 such "colleges" were estimated to have opened their doors in the United States during the 19th century, more than a quarter of them between 1875 and 1890. Some didn't get much beyond the issuance of a prospectus; others graduated a class or two and then collapsed. In some areas the schools were heavily concentrated. The state of Missouri alone had more than 40; Illinois almost as many. Cincinnati boasted 20 and Chicago more than a dozen; Louisville, Kentucky, wasn't far behind.

Generally, a two-year course of instruction was ad-

(Above) Before 1890 most doctors of the Old West started practice without a glance into a microscope, though the instrument had been available for many years. Laboratory classes like the one shown here helped immensely in the upgrading of the profession. (Left) Medical journals were vital to the dissemination of knowledge. Many doctors, who were originally ill-trained, made up for their deficiencies by voracious reading.

Northwest Medicine, "100 Years of Medical Education in Oregon"

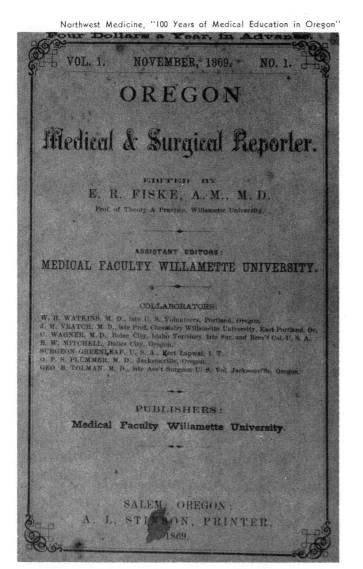

vertised—but in practice, the schools were in session no more than four or five months out of 12. Besides that, the curriculum of the second year was merely a repeat of the first. Some schools had a skeleton or two for demonstration purposes; others got by with just a box of bones. There were no laboratories to speak of, and libraries were woefully meager. The results, of course, were obvious. Physicians with only a modicum of training marched out into the world—and for many of them, that meant the excitement of the vibrant West.

In many respects, the pioneer doctor is even *more* deserving of his perch on the pedestal of history. After all, so many of them started out with so much still to learn. Legal restrictions and religious objections to autopsies and against the use of cadavers for study particularly limited the training for surgery and internal medicine. Almost none of the schools had affiliations with hospitals so that students could get a little first-hand experience. In other words, the young graduates were shown a few basic strokes, forced out onto a medical diving board and told to sink or swim!

In a period when patent potions and flagrant quackery were widely accepted, the new "diploma doctors" were not questioned; in fact, they were considered highly proficient by the simple standard of comparison—to medicine men or "granny" practitioners. It was after they hung their shingle and went to work on their own that the doctors themselves became aware of their educational shortcomings. And it was out of this awareness that the first movements for reform began to generate.

Wherever several medical doctors of serious intent congregated, they soon were meeting to discuss the formation of an association—to advance the causes and knowledge of their profession, to eliminate the unworthy and to banish the quack. Education and licensing were heated topics. In the Old West—until territories and states were created—legal restrictions were virtually non-existent, and, in many places, a doctor was a doctor simply if he said he was. Forged diplomas were not uncommon. Horse doctors treated people, so did a shoemaker in Empire City, Oregon; a fisherman in Cloverdale, California; a porter in Brownsville, Texas, and a barber in South Dakota. Circuit-riding ministers often carried a medicine kit. There were scores of faith-healers and "irregulars" of all kinds. Many pharmacists had extensive medical practices—not necessarily because they wanted to, but because they were the only ones available with any know-how whatsoever.

It was more than half a century before all the western states had official medical associations, but as early as 1853 the doctors of Minnesota and Texas had their professional societies organized. Three years later California physicians drew up their by-laws in Sacramento, and the new *California State Medical Journal* in 1856 editorialized: ". . . in no country is there a greater proportion of unscrupulous and murderous pretenders to be unmasked and driven from their unholy and reckless tampering with human life."

Still, it was ten years before the California legislature passed its first medical-practice law. Three years earlier—in 1873—Texas became the first state to establish a board of medical examiners. The new statutes which followed in other areas, however, did not automatically create a medical utopia. Examining boards began to weed out a few unworthy candidates, but from state to state there was little uniformity in tests

The Toland Medical College was founded in San Francisco, California, in 1864 by Dr. Hugh H. Toland. It was the forerunner of the University of California Medical School.

In 1865 the requirements for gradution were:

1. The candidate must be 21 years of age.
2. He must have attended two full courses of Medical lectures, one of which must have been delivered in this Institution.
3. He must have attended a course of practical anatomy in the dissecting room.
4. The candidate must have studied medicine for three years (the terms of attending lectures included) under the direction of a respectable medical practitioner.
5. He must write a Medical Thesis and submit the same to the Faculty two weeks prior to the Commencement.

The school prospectus further advised that "there is no climate, perhaps in the world, which has a more invigorating effect upon persons coming from the interior of our States and Territories, thereby qualifying the votaries of study with essential health and inspiration. . . . In winter or summer, dissections can be made without detriment to the health of the student."

or regulations—and, unfortunately, enforcement of the laws of licensure was extremely difficult. In a few instances, skulduggery was involved in the testing process, answers being sold in advance to candidates or to a "diploma mill" so it could prepare its students for the examination. Then, too, there was the necessity for "grandfather clauses," to permit preceptor-trained doc-

Improved schools and better instructors were continuing demands of early medical associations. An outstanding surgeon who trained many western practitioners was Dr. Nicholas Senn (below). He was an instructor at the Rush Medical School in Chicago (bottom). At right is Waller Hall at Willamette University, Salem, Oregon, where medical students started training in the basement in 1867.

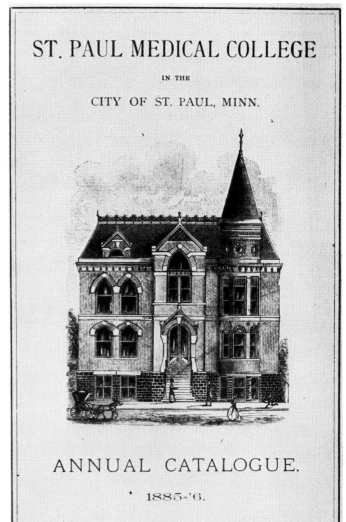

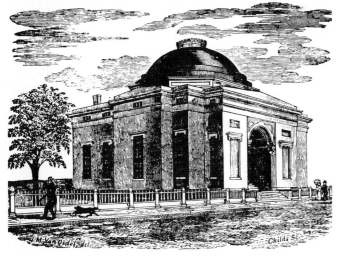

ST. PAUL MEDICAL COLLEGE

IN THE

CITY OF ST. PAUL, MINN.

ANNUAL CATALOGUE.

1885-'6.

60

The Omaha (Neb.) Medical College was housed in this wooden structure in 1887 when this photo was taken. The sign on the building says "Free Dispensary," which was one method of giving medical students practical experience. It was this lack which marked the era of the "diploma mills." Dr. William F. Milroy stood at the entrance.

tors of long experience to qualify for a state license. Again, loopholes permitted a few quacks and irregulars to slip through.

But out of this somewhat chaotic situation, a semblance of order began to occur in the final quarter of the 19th century. The American Medical Association—in official existence from 1847—did what it could to foster standardization in the far reaches of the frontier. The appearance of legitimate schools, which would one day become part of major universities, was a harbinger of better things ahead. In California, the Medical Department of the University of the Pacific was founded in 1859; it later became the Cooper Medical School and finally the Stanford University School of

61

Medicine. In 1864 Toland Medical School was established in San Francisco, the forerunner of the University of California Medical School.

Three years later in Salem, Oregon, the Medical Department of Willamette University announced its first lecture series. Like the profession itself, the school's history was marked with dissension and divided opinions, culminating in 1887 with a mass resignation of faculty members. That same year four of the "rebel" doctors acquired a charter for the University of Oregon Medical School which they opened in Portland in a former grocery store. (Cadavers were hauled to the second-story dissecting room by block-and-tackle). In

Licensure was a continuing bone of contention for pioneer practitioners. In many places one became a doctor simply by saying he was one; it was the perfect seed-bed for quackery. The creation of state boards of medical examiners (Oregon's first in 1889 is pictured below) began the difficult task of weeding out the charlatans and the poorly trained. "Grandfather clauses" and examination skulduggery permitted a few frauds and third-raters to slip through, but in time most of the loopholes were patched. Left to right were Drs. James Dickson, James Brown and O. P. S. Plummer.

Northwest Medicine "100 Years of Medical Education in Oregon"

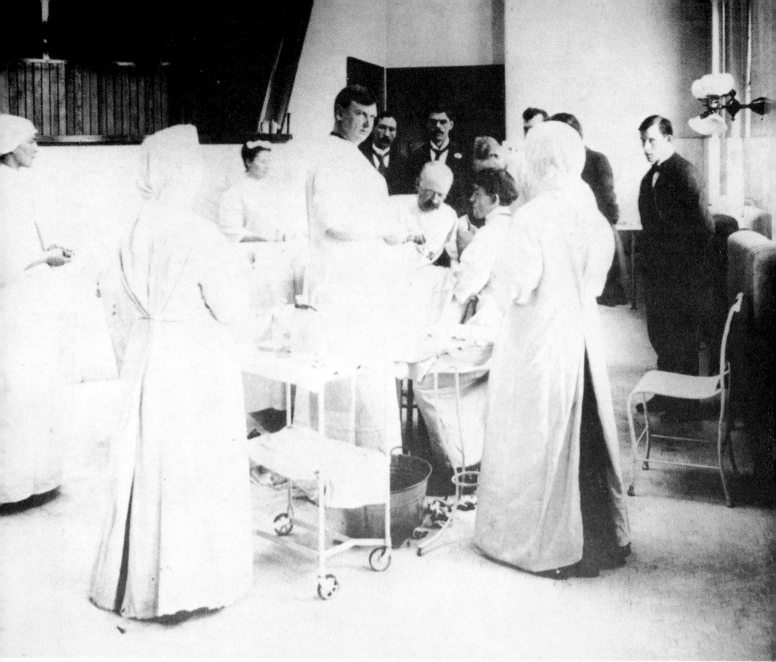

Minnesota Historical Society

time the earlier animosities were forgotten, and in 1913 the Willamette Medical Department was consolidated with the Portland institution.

So it was that the country doctors and the saddlebag surgeons learned their skills. Obviously, they ranged the complete spectrum of ability and knowledge because they came from such a varied background of training and philosophy. Out of this medical melange, however, evolved a professional unity which rose above the charlatans and montebanks. But people being gullible as they are, quackery never did disappear; it merely changed its form, and each new generation can recite its version of the medieval dirge:

The times are ominous indeed,
When quack to quack cries, "purge and bleed."

(Above) This 1890 operation in St. Luke's Hospital, St. Paul, Minnesota, was a far cry from the kitchen-table surgery of a few years earlier. Actually, the latter was to exist in some places until the third decade of the 20th century. (Below) Dr. Christian Fenger—shown performing an autopsy in the Cook County (Ill.) morgue—was one of the nation's outstanding teachers as a new era dawned in medical education.

Mayo Clinic, Rochester, Minnesota

(Opposite page) This doctor in Garden City, Kansas, had rugs on the floor and a canopied bed in his combination office and surgery. The availability of a nurse and an assistant was a special luxury which few country physicians enjoyed. (Above) More typical were the quarters of Dr. John W. Thompson in Sutton, Nebraska.

Tools, Techniques and Aching Teeth

He is the best physician who knows how to distinguish the possible from the impossible.

HEROPHILUS

STARTING practice in a frontier community was a relatively simple matter; surviving the physical strains and making it pay were something else again.

When a young physician arrived in a mining settlement or a prairie boom-town, he followed a rather general process. If a registration law was in effect (and it seldom was until later years), he would show his diploma to the local clerk, pay a small fee and sign up. If not, he simply went about the business of finding an office on which to hang his shingle.

A drugstore was an ideal location, and if the town didn't already have one, the doctor took care of that by starting his own. It gave him a second source of income, and it solved his office and supply problems. Then came a visit to the newspaper publisher.

Usually the doctor bought a small professional announcement, but in the early days the ethics of medical advertising were not always rigidly followed. For instance, the Wichita, Kansas, *Eagle* in 1872 carried a card which read: "Dr. A. J. Goggins, late of New York City, treats venereal disease as a specialty, and your secret is the doctor's secret."

Dr. Frank Pottle advertised in the *Great Falls* (Mont.) *Tribune* that he would "give one hundred dollars to any case of Rheumatism, La Grippe, Neuralgia or any other disease originating from a cold that he

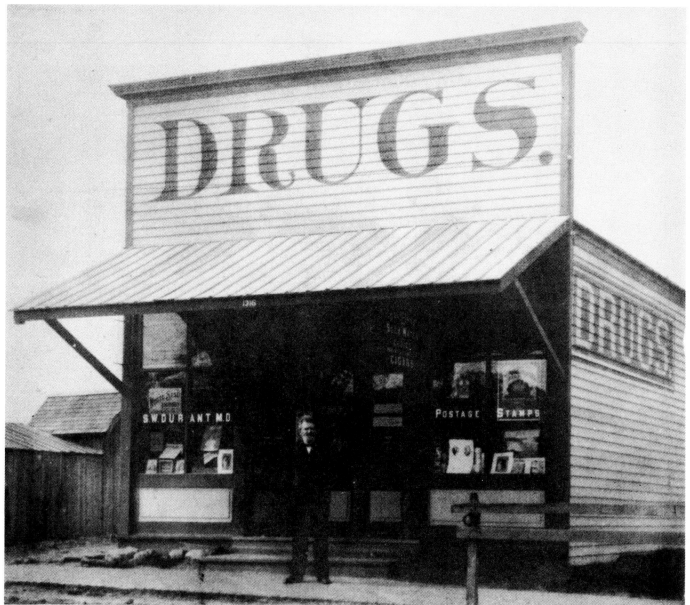

Early-day physicians often doubled as pharmacists. Typical was Dr. S. W. Durant who operated this drugstore in Topeka, Kansas. The stores provided a headquarters, a second source of income and a ready supply of drugs and medicines. One of the incongruities, though, was the fact that many doctor-owned stores sold the quack nostrums which the physicians themselves decried.

can't cure." Dr. S. S. Marsters of Little Shasta, California, boasted in print in 1871 that he could save anyone suffering any case of fever or inflammation of the chest or abdomen—or he would "advertise the fatal result six months in the *Yreka Journal*." (He didn't indicate what benefit that might be to the victim!) Some doctors put it succinctly: "Recovery guaranteed or no pay."

For equipment the pioneer practitioner often got started with the barest minimum. After the Civil War, "army surplus" surgical instruments in velvet-lined field cases turned up in increasing numbers on the western frontier. So did small medicine kits with tiny vials for a variety of decoctions which the doctor might need for any emergency. If he traveled by horse-

back, he got a medical saddlebag which sold for as much as twelve dollars. For his town calls and buggy trips he used a leather satchel.

The stethoscope was invented in 1819 by Rene Theophile Laennec when he rolled up a sheet of writing paper so that he could better hear the cardiac impulses of a particularly plump woman. A crude wooden instrument was later developed and became part of the country doctor's working paraphernalia, though many preferred the old-fashioned method of placing an ear directly against the patient's chest.

Though there were surplus field microscopes available after the Civil War, most small-town doctors got along without them. The same was true of other refinements, including special chairs and tables in their offices for examinations and treatment. Rudimentary furnishings were a heating stove, a bowl-and-pitcher, a "slop jar" and a roll-top desk. Occasionally the waiting room and office were one and the same, a condition which didn't especially appeal to the more timid patients.

More important were the physician's knowledge, his native ability, his adaptability to unusual circumstances and his inventive genius. Frontier doctors treated frontier people under frontier conditions, so it was not a matter of fancy equipment, but what could

Surplus medical equipment from the Civil War was in considerable evidence on the western frontier. Later the eastern manufacturers recognized a growing market and began to turn out saddlebags, surgical kits and other equipment adapted to the needs of the horse-and-buggy practitioners.

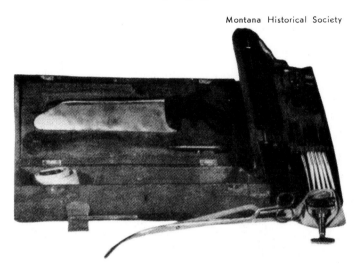

DOSING AND DROPPING BOTTLES.

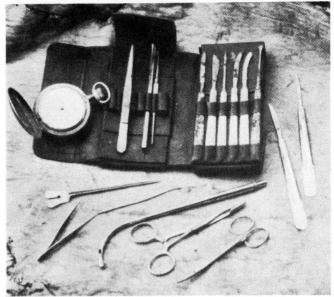

(Above) The Kansas State Historical Society
(Opposite page) State Historical Society of Colorado

(Opposite page) Dr. James Raizon, at left, consulted in this much-cluttered office in Trinidad, Colorado. (Above) Normally, pioneer doctors advertised with professional dignity in their local newspapers, but sometimes they got carried away.

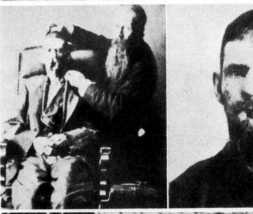

be accomplished with what was available. Ranch work shops and farm kitchens were regularly the scene of medical ingenuity. In addition to making special apparatus from fence wire and household utensils, pioneer doctors were known to have searched the fields and stream banks for drug-bearing plants needed in a particular emergency.

The locale usually had much to do with the frequency of certain ailments and injuries. In gold-rush shack towns, railroad construction camps and the ubiquitous "hog ranches," physicians were forever patching up the results of saloon brawls or trying to undo the damages of amorous relationships with ladies of easy virtue. When settlements developed more permanently and families arrived, the incidence of violence and riotous living decreased while care of ailing children increased.

In the cold-winter country, frostbite was a constant problem, and amputations were frequent. When min-

Picture credits (top to bottom): (Ruth Herold) The Seattle Times; Western History Research Center, University of Wyoming; Northern Pacific Railway.

(Top) Surgical kit belonging to Dr. Alex de Soto, who practiced at the turn of the century in Seattle, Washington. (Center) Pioneer doctors were willing to try—often without precedent. Dr. Thomas G. Maghee of Rawlins, Wyoming Territory, chloroformed a sheepherder 39 times in 1886-87 while he patiently rebuilt a face which had been almost shot away. (Bottom) Amputations, however, were the order of the day, mostly because the physicians didn't know how to effect a cure any other way.

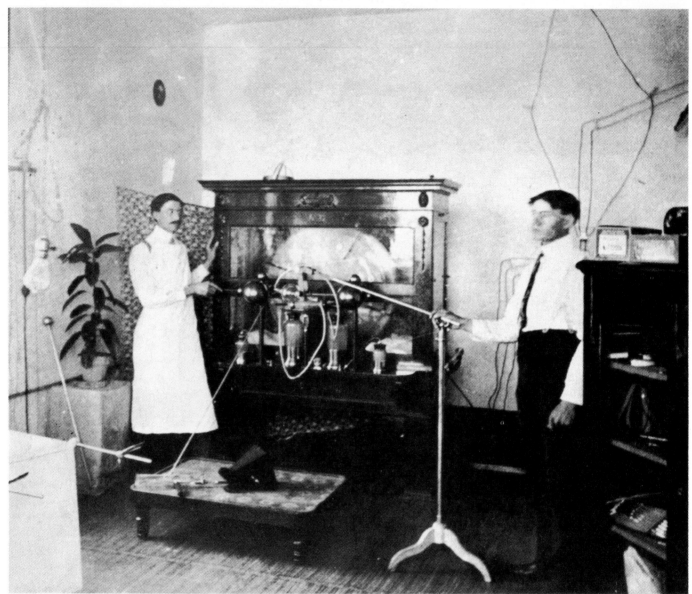

(Dr. E. S. Lain Collection) Division of Manuscripts, University of Oklahoma

Wilhelm Roentgen's X-ray brought a new dimension to the practice of medicine. It introduced a modern era when doctors no longer had to depend upon their simple manual instruments, nearly all of which they could carry in a small satchel. The static glass-plate model above was owned by Dr. E. S. Lain in Oklahoma. The Static X-Ray Machine manufactured by the Betz Company in 1905 (illustrated in the sketch below) also included an "ozone outfit, a cataphoric outfit and a Morton Wave."

St. Louis Medical Society

ers went underground, eye injuries from flying rock became a continuing hazard. Cowboys—in spite of their historic reputation for horsemanship—were regularly treated for broken bones caused by uncooperative mounts. Where rattlesnakes abounded, doctors carried ammonia as a neutralizer; to some old-timers, though, a pair of fresh fang marks afforded a splendid excuse for an over-dose of whiskey, always the favorite remedy of the frontier whether it worked or not.

Epidemics of all kinds were feared by doctors and the citizenry alike. Cholera was a particularly vicious killer along the trails to the West. Whole families were wiped out by a contagion which no physician of the period truly understood. A few early exponents of san-

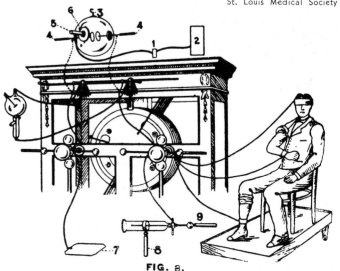

FIG. 8.

Static electricity devices were used by both legitimate doctors and quacks. While the mountebanks of medicine were claiming all sorts of miracle cures for an assortment of wierd apparatuses, physicians were employing them cautiously as muscle stimulators, relaxers and nerve-soothers. The machine at right offered the distinct advantage that no disrobing was necessary, and that it could deliver all the benefits derived from manual massage.

In the photo below, Dr. and Mrs. Alexander Barkley are shown operating their new X-ray machine in Hobart, Oklahoma. In the early days, lack of knowledge of the X-ray resulted in numerous cases of overexposure as physicians experimented with a device which proved to be far more than a medical plaything.

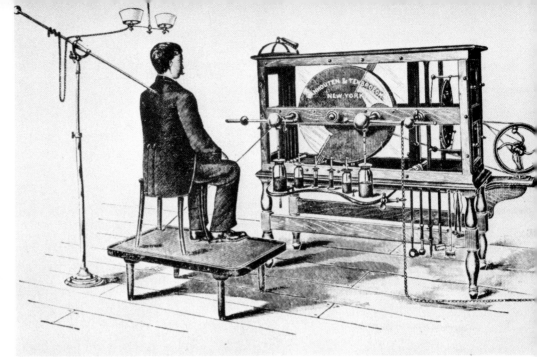

itation were basically on the right track—but they didn't know why. Meanwhile, polluted water holes and diseased campsites continued to claim a heavy toll, and Indians—digging up buried victims for their clothing—spread the scourge to their highly susceptible tribesmen. Red pepper in whiskey was a folk remedy even the doctors used. When an epidemic hit Ft. Riley, Kansas, in 1855, a physician frantically burned barrels of pine tar beneath open hospital windows because he didn't know what else to do.

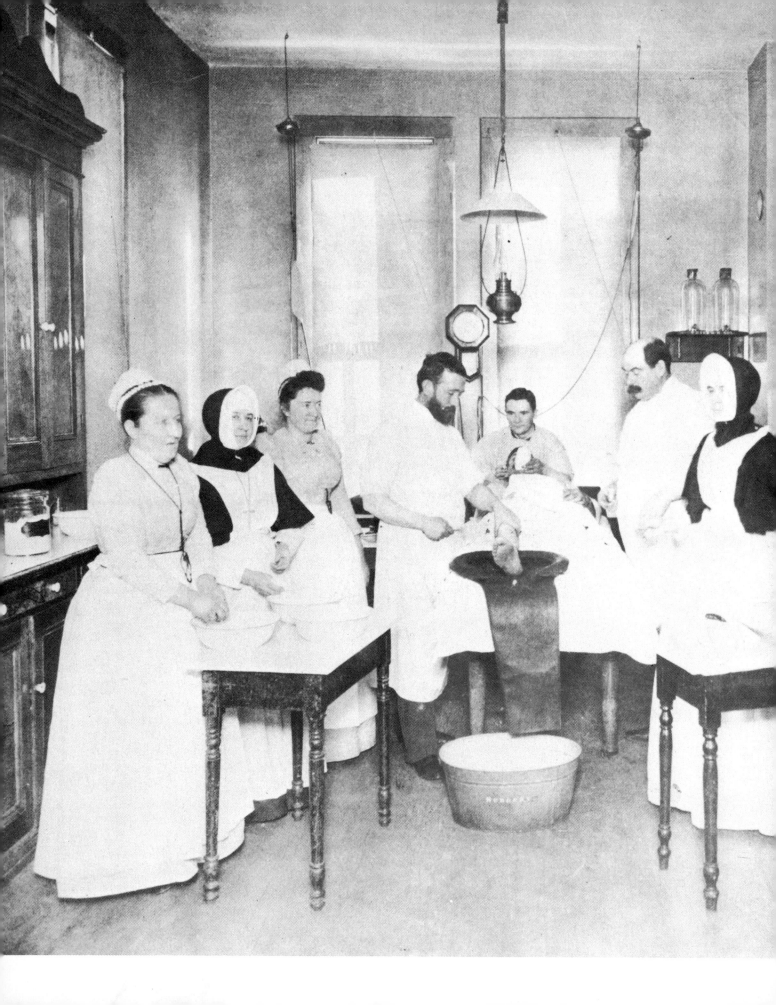

Smallpox spread terror wherever it struck, but at least it was possible to vaccinate for it, and in some communities doctors volunteered to immunize everyone free. Fear, ignorance and apathy combined to prevent any widespread protection, however. Malaria (the ague) was seemingly everywhere, and influenza (grippe) struck periodically. More disastrous—especially to young children—were epidemics of whooping cough and diphtheria. Physicians tried valiantly with limited resources to cope with the attacks. For diphtheria, sulphur or powdered brimstone boiled in lime-water was dropped into the patient's nostrils with a quill. In some cases throats were opened and attempts made to suck out the congestion. Another treatment was to hold the suffering youngster upside down while his throat was tickled with a feather soaked in goose grease, with the hope that he would vomit up the offending substance.

There were so many forms of fever that they were continually confused in diagnosis and treatment. Tuberculosis, pneumonia and rheumatism were commonplace, either brought on or aggravated by living conditions in sod houses and drafty log huts or by too much exposure to the elements.

So it was that the pioneer doctor had his hands full, but there was one thing about him: he wasn't afraid to try! Dr. Pablo Saler, the surgeon at Monterey, California, from 1791 to 1800, scooped up the intestines of an Indian gored by a bull, replaced them deftly and stitched up the wound. According to the *Montana Post*

(At left) This dramatic old photo shows surgery as it used to be, complete with wash tub and Kelly pad. The picture was taken at St. Vincent's Hospital in Portland, Oregon. (Below) Still another example of pre-1900 surgery revealed little care given to antiseptic condition.

(At left) Northwest Medicine, "100 Years of Medical Education in Oregon"

(Below) Harborview (King County) Hospital, Seattle, Washington

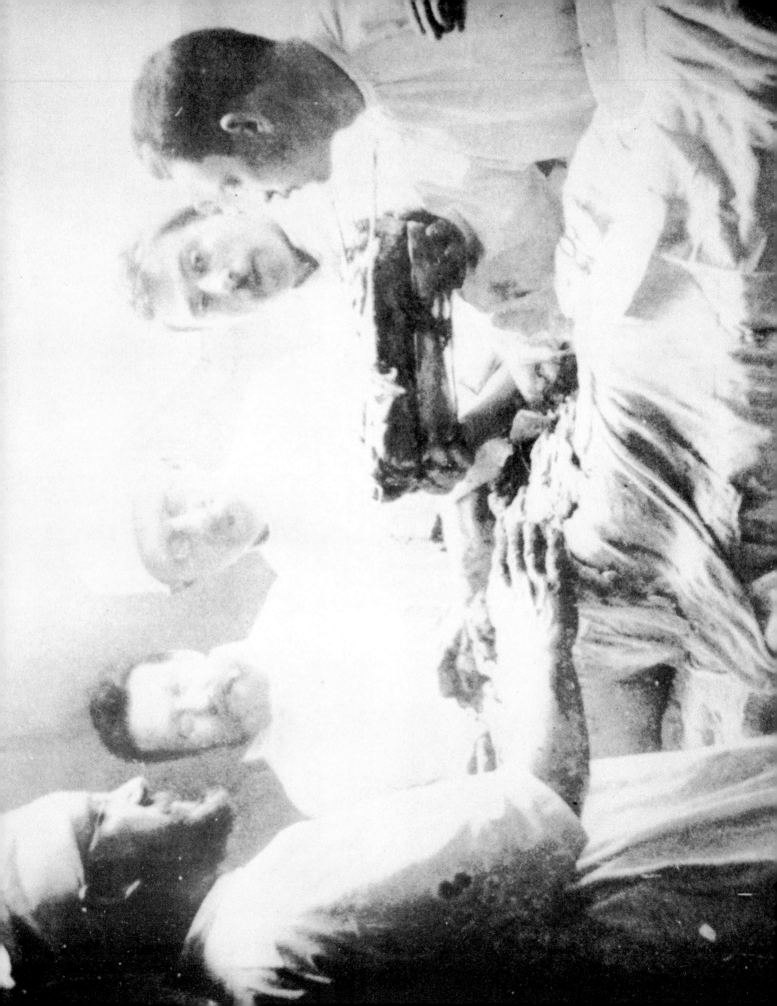

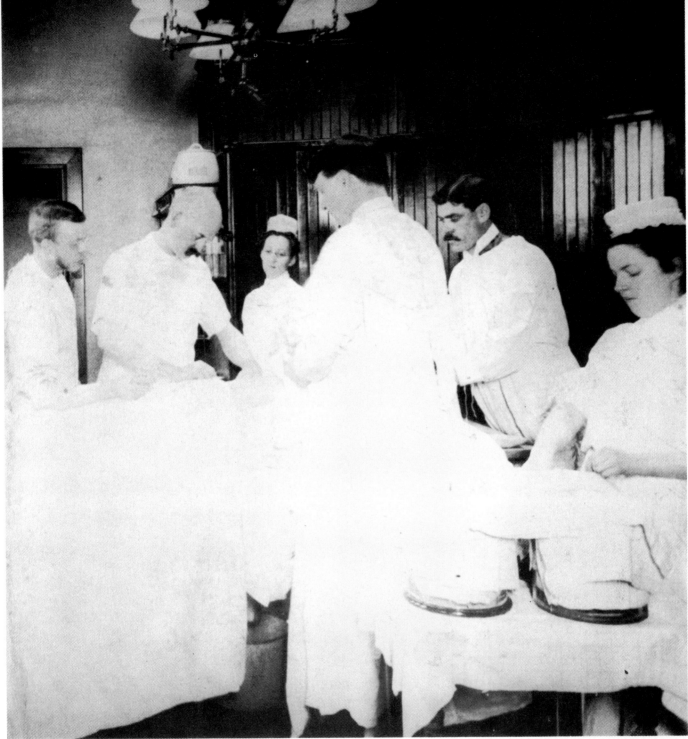

(Opposite page) Ramsey County (Minnesota) Medical Society

(Above) Minnesota Historical Society

(Opposite page) It was difficult to break old habits in medicine. While Listerian operations were coming into vogue, many surgeons objected to the drenching by carbolic acid sprays and other "inconveniences" necessitated by new-fangled ideas of antisepsis. One doctor in this group even held firmly to his cigar. (Above) In the late 1800s, as the "old breed"—the Civil War and outpost practitioners—began to disappear, the transition to new ideas picked up tempo. No longer were needles stuck in the lapels of Prince Albert coats or scalpels held in the mouth while hands were busy. The frontier was a thing of the past—and so was frontier medicine.

of December 12, 1866, Dr. Jerome S. Glick removed a 70-foot tapeworm from a patient in Virginia City. Another Montana physician, Dr. R. P. R. Gordon, operated for hernia at a remote sheep ranch, using turpentine as the antiseptic.

That, of course, wasn't exactly what Joseph Lister

had in mind when he introduced his carbolic acid system of antisepsis in 1867. Appreciation of sanitation and cleanliness was slow in coming, and it took almost two decades before Listerian operations were regularly practiced in the United States. Habits of generations were difficult to break, and doctors occasionally were

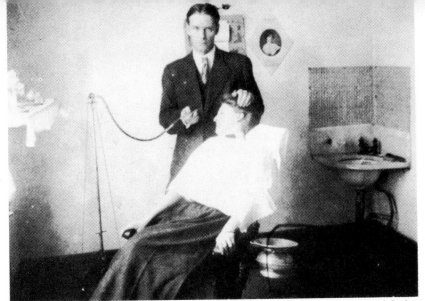

J. P. M. BURKET, M. D., D. D. S.,
DENTIST,
KINGMAN, - - - KANSAS:

Will visit Cheney the first and third Monday's in each month. Prepared to do all kinds of Dental work. All work warranted by Dr. Burket. Office at Tyler House, Main street. Dr. J. T. Baird, of Wichita, an experienced Dentist, will visit Cheney in Dr. Burket's absence.

Dr. Burket has had twenty years experience as a physician. Cures all blood and skin diseases, kidney and bladder trouble, and all diseases of the urinary organs. Private diseases speedily cured. Females successfully treated of all diseases peculiar to their sex. Consultation free and invited. Will visit Cheney once a month in person.

The Kansas State Historical Society

Clackamas County (Oregon) Historical Society

Dentistry had a slower development as a full-fledged profession than did medicine. In pioneer days, dental work—which was mostly a matter of pulling teeth—was done by a physician as an extra-curricular chore. Occasionally, doctors held both degrees—dental and medical—as J. P. M. Burket advertised in Kingman, Kansas.

among the worst offenders in the area of antiseptic precautions. Some surgeons washed their hands *after* an operation and not before. While they were working, they kept needles stuck in their coat lapels and wiped their hands on their trousers. A few even smoked cigars.

It was a paradoxical era. Some of the same men who were trying so hard to keep patients alive were oblivious to the basic rules of sanitation—not because they didn't care, but more because they didn't *know*. In Tucson, Arizona, for instance, Dr. John C. Handy, who was humanitarian enough to offer free smallpox vaccinations to those who could not pay, at the same time piped the sewage from his house into the street. When city officials closed the outlet, the doctor sued.

Gradually, though, the awakening came. Germs were accepted as a scientific reality and not a far-fetched theory. More and more research was conducted; medical knowledge grew; and life expectancy increased. Soddies and log cabins were replaced by more healthful dwellings. Food was generally more abundant and more nourishing. Condensed milk, for example, was a revolutionary product for the feeding of babies. The almost-primitive medicine practiced in the western wilderness in the early 1800s slowly evolved into a

modern science as the final years of the century slipped away.

Surgery especially became a far-cry from the bowie knife probings on the frontier, but there were new developments at every turn. In December of 1895 Wilhelm Conrad Roentgen, a German physicist, gave the world an exciting new Christmas present: the X-ray. The reception was startling. In London a firm began selling X-ray-proof underwear. The state of New York

(Opposite page) Montana Historical Society

(Right) (N. H. Rose Collection)
Division of Manuscripts, University of Oklahoma Library

(Opposite page) In the march of progress, gases such as nitrous oxide joined the list of pioneer anesthetics like whiskey and chloroform. This photo was taken in the office of Dr. Joseph Hunter at Boulder Hot Springs, Montana. (Right) John Henry (Doc) Holliday, gunman and gambler of the Old West, was not a physician—and he is included here merely to dispel again that persistent fallacy. Before he went to Tombstone, Arizona, Holliday practiced dentistry briefly. After a notorious high-living career, he died of tuberculosis in his mid-thirties.

77

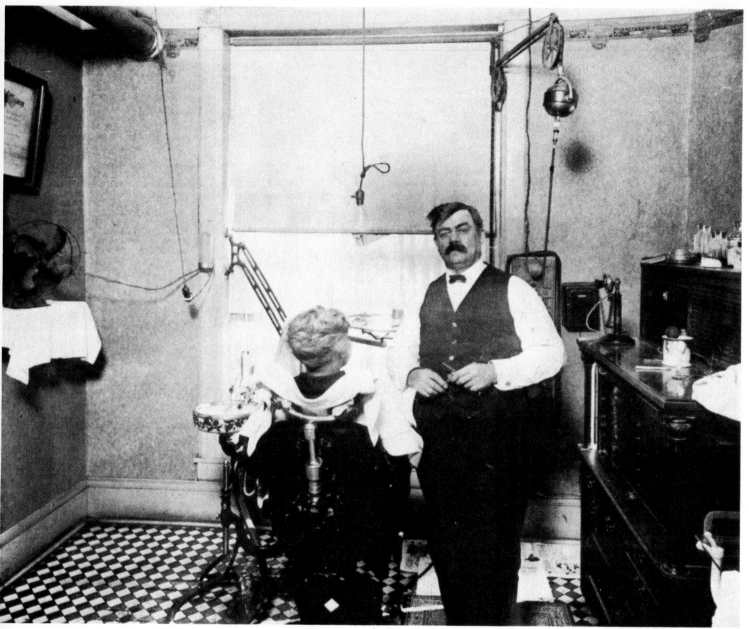

Dr. R. H. Pendleton had all the modern conveniences—an electric fan, an electric light, an electric drill, a stand-up telephone and a tilt-back chair. By the turn of the century dentistry had come a long way from the days when patent medicine hawkers pulled teeth free to draw a crowd.

tried to pass legislation banning the discovery in opera glasses. But the defenders of international modesty relaxed when the limitations of the device became better known. More positive, however, were the reactions of many physicians, including Dr. J. Grosvenor Cross, who had an X-ray machine in his office in Rochester, Minnesota, within two months after Roentgen's announcement. At first it was virtually a medical toy, and then came his perfect chance to demonstrate its value. A youngster had swallowed a belt buckle and was rushed to the Mayo brothers. They were concerned about removal because they didn't know exactly which direction its prongs were facing, so they took the child

to Doctor Cross. His pictures clearly outlined the buckle; it was pointed so that removing it through the mouth would have been seriously dangerous. So Dr. Charles Mayo operated with complete knowledge, and extracted the buckle, blunt end first.

This, of course, was merely an isolated incident, but it portrayed graphically the progress which had been made in a short period of years.

Meanwhile, there was another phase of the pioneer doctor's career which deserves mention. In many areas of the western frontier, dentists were rare, if not non-existent. So by default rather than by choice, local physicians (and a few druggists, too) got into the tooth-pulling business. At that time, little thought was given to saving a tooth; if a cowboy had an aching molar, he wanted it out—no matter what he had to suffer in the process. Country doctors often carried a special turnbuckle device—reminiscent of the Inquisition—with which they accommodated their dental patients.

Itinerant dentists occasionally visited a community, setting up shop for a week or so, during which time they extracted all the bad teeth which had accumulated since their last trip. Dr. Urling C. Coe, a pioneer physician in Oregon, periodically conducted a tooth-pulling "bee" at one of the ranches in his territory. Word of the event would get around, and all the ranch hands with dental problems would gather at the appointed place. While the doctor had a busy day with the forceps, the cowboys would drink lots of whiskey—before the operation for courage, and after in celebration!

In time, most settlements of any size had a full-time dentist, and the country doctor was relieved of his extra-curricular chore. The frontier physician lived and worked in an era of versatility. He was—for lack of a better phrase—a medical jack-of-all-trades.

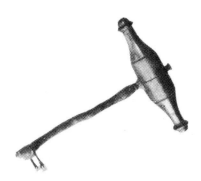

Frontier physicians often carried a turnbuckle like the one above to pull teeth in emergencies. By 1900 the equipment of dentistry had become far more sophisticated as indicated by Dr. Harvey Blain's office (below left). In Stillwater, Oklahoma Territory, Dr. E. L. Moore prepared for an extraction (below right) while his patient held on for dear life.

Sharlot Hall Historical Museum of Arizona, Prescott

(Oklahoma State Dental Association Collection)
Division of Manuscripts, University of Oklahoma Library

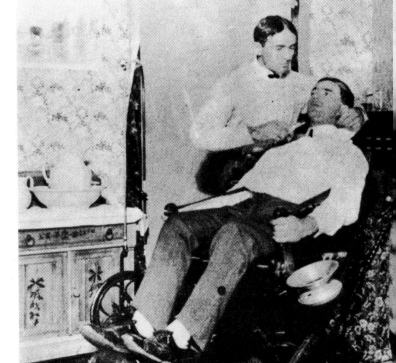

(Opposite page) Shepard Ambulance Service, Seattle, Washington   (Above) Utah State Historical Society

In the 19th century horses played the major role in medical logistics. "Horse-and-buggy doctor" became an accepted phrase, descriptive of the pioneer physician who took his talents to his patients. Dr. John F. Hamilton of Salt Lake City (above) typified the era in his high-wheeled phaeton. As hospitals developed and home practice started to decline, a need for ambulance service grew accordingly. In Portland, Oregon, the Hoffman & Shepard Company provided medical transportation (opposite page).

From Shank's Mare to Stanley Steamers

Don't spare the horses when a human life is at stake.

WILLIAM WORRALL MAYO, M.D.

A COUNTRY doctor's practice offered two distinct challenges: how to get to his patient, and what to do after he got there! Often the former was the more difficult of the two.

It is somewhat unusual that the spotlight of nostalgia has tended to focus on the country doctor's buggy or "matching blacks" rather than on his professional skill or personal achievements. Somehow, though, the memoirs and diaries of Old West pioneers invariably recall how the contemporary physician made his rounds—but little of what he accomplished. Possibly it was because they, too, knew the rigors of a 30-mile

horseback ride through the bitter cold and almost nothing about the ministrations of a doctor at an ailing patient's bedside.

Even more interesting, however, is that the old-time practitioners, too, wrote more in later years about their horses than the results of their services. They forgot

(Dr. Lewis J. Moorman Collection)
Division of Manuscripts, University of Oklahoma Library

Country doctors were often called into virtually road-less territory to visit the sick. The horse-and-buggy provided the most reliable means for such cross-country travel.

81

the names of patients whose lives they saved, but they always remembered "Mingo" or "Black Jack" when they penned their recollections for posterity.

Illnesses—particularly the respiratory kind—quite often came when the weather was bad. It was then that the country doctor was summoned to make long and hazardous trips through swirling snows or icy spring floods, and it was then that a good horse or team meant so much to him. More than one M.D. owed his longevity to the homing instincts of a horse which managed to make it back to the barn when trails were obliterated and a blizzard howled.

There were other times, too, when a doctor gave his horse free rein. After a particularly wearisome journey with little or no sleep, the return trek was a good time to take a much-needed nap while "Old Nell" plodded relentlessly homeward. On other occasions when the weather was nice, a country practitioner might be seen in his buggy reading a medical text, oblivious to the surroundings while his horse was in full charge of navigation.

In a saddle, of course, there was little to do but ride and think, (though some doctors claimed they could sleep there, too). A fast pony was a decided advantage when speed was required and most early-day practitioners kept their medical saddlebags packed for a periodic race against death. Dr. Dennis M. Parker of Billings, Montana, once was said to have ridden 70

(Above) In derby and high collar, Dr. Frederick Teal, a pioneer Nebraska physician, posed with his partner-in-medicine. (Below) Most early-day practitioners were equally at home in the saddle. In this picture Dr. Fred Horton of Newcastle, Wyoming, was on a hunting mission. Many doctors carried guns in their buggies, and occasionally brought in a deer or a brace of prairie chickens after a country call.

miles to treat a gunshot victim. As soon as it was possible, though, most doctors switched to buggies, buckboards or carts because they could carry more equipment, and the exhaustion factor wasn't so great.

In his reminiscences, Dr. George O. A. Kellogg of Nampa, Idaho, wrote:

"I used my single driver within a radius of three or four miles, a livery team within a distance of 40 miles and Wells-Fargo and privately-owned stage lines for greater distances. I had my own heavy mountain buggy which I kept packed with sterile supplies and equipment, including fishing tackle, shotgun and rifle. I would add my surgical bag and obstetrical bag and

Mrs. Lewis J. Moorman

(Above) Dr. Lewis J. Moorman credited his horse, "Old Billy," with "intuitive sagacity" as they teamed up to bring medical service to the settlers around Jet, Oklahoma. (Left) A bicycle was used for town calls by Dr. Frederick J. McNulty of Yreka, California. He used a buggy, too, and once took a load of barley in payment of an amputation fee.

Siskiyou County Museum, Yreka, California

medicine case and be prepared for any emergency."

Dr. Arthur E. Hertzler, who practiced on the plains of Kansas, added some extra gear: a Colt "Peacemaker" for protection, a kerosene lantern, a scoop shovel to dig out of snowdrifts, a hammer and wire-cutters. In Oklahoma Dr. Benjamin P. Magness always included a "cattleman's friend," a combination staple-puller, wire-stretcher, cutter, pliers and hammer. Through he snipped many fence wires so he could take cross-country short-cuts, he boasted that he always repaired the damage before he traveled on.

Though two-wheeled carts were faster and less cumbersome, pioneer physicians seemed to show a

In his saddlebags the country doctor carried his pharmacy and his limited equipment. He had to travel light because it was not unusual for him to ride more than 50 miles to treat an emergency case. In many areas a total lack of roads made horseback the logical means of transportation.

(Above) Dr. John C. Handy was one of Arizona Territory's pioneer physicians. A graduate of Cooper Medical College in 1863, the fiery-tempered doctor made it his personal business to challenge the credentials of other medical practitioners who came to the Tucson area. (Below) Dr. Andrew Fabrique used a single horse rig for country calls around Wichita, Kansas.

preference for four-wheeled vehicles. Carts were far less comfortable, and they had a tendency to upset or throw a dozing doctor out when they hit a rut or rock. On the other hand, the two-wheelers were better for off-road travel and for dodging mud holes and other obstacles—if the driver stayed constantly alert.

Some practices covered several counties, so it was not uncommon for a doctor to travel by train when it was feasible. In earlier days "canoe doctors" like Charles Hadley Spinning and Clarence A. Smith of Washington Territory made countless journeys over

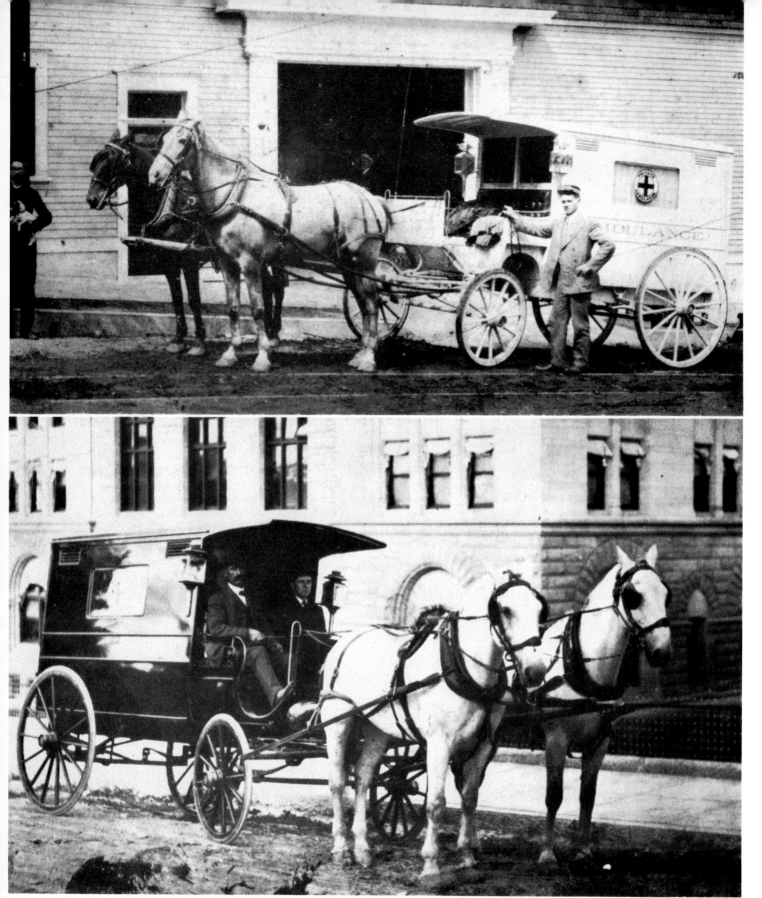

(Top) Shepard Ambulance Service, Seattle, Washington   (Bottom) Montana Historical Society

Early-day ambulances were not quite as exciting as horse-drawn fire engines of the same era, but they made a dramatic appearance wherever they went because of the emergency nature of their mission. (Above) Frank Shepard operated ambulances in Portland, Oregon, and Seattle, Washington. (Below) The Helena Cab Company provided the medical transportation in that Montana city in 1895.

water to treat ailing Indians and white settlers. Dr. Frederick A. Churchill of Seattle added a small compass to his instrument bag after he and the frantic husband of a patient spent all night trying to row to Mercer Island—and ended up on the wrong side of Lake Washington when dawn disclosed their position.

For town calls, a bicycle was sometimes used. Doctor Hertzler in his memoirs said that it was difficult for a physician to maintain his dignity while pedaling up the street, especially if he were long and gangly. Mules, the same doctor believed, were equally unbecoming to the profession, though he used them himself when the going got especially rough. Another physician—an exponent of bicycles—actually advertised that he could be at the patient's door while his old-fashioned competitors were still harnessing up. Professional dignity meant nothing to Dr. Edwin W. Bathurst of

Saint Joseph Hospital, Denver, Colorado

(Above) In Denver, Colorado, Saint Joseph Hospital was providing horse-drawn ambulance service at the turn of the century. (Below) In Minneapolis, Minnesota, a police ambulance made an emergency stop at the Hotel Atlantic while the morbid curious gathered.

(Luxton Collection) Minnesota Historical Society

Siskiyou County, California, who donned snowshoes to make winter calls in the mountains, and once he swam the raging Salmon River and walked six miles in wet clothes to treat an injured miner.

Summoning the doctor in an era of limited communications facilities was not always an easy task. Quite often a youngster, a worried husband or the patient's neighbor galloped into town on a lathered horse with a confused tale of symptoms and dire fears. Some practitioners had an outdoor bell system rigged up so that their wives could signal them in such emergencies. Of course, everyone else knew that "Doc" had a hurry-up case when the bell rang, and tongues wagged until the details were known.

Before Rochester, Minnesota, had a telephone

Sedgwick County (Kansas) Medical Society

(Above right) Wichita, Kansas, had rubber-tired ambulance service in 1890. Black horses were hitched to the same vehicle and it became a hearse. (Below) Wicker baskets were commonly used for morgue pickups. This dramatic picture was taken in Minneapolis, Minnesota, following a murder in 1900.

(Luxton Collection) Minnesota Historical Society

Many pioneer doctors were bicycle-riders. A few, however, believed that it was an undignified form of transportation for a professional man. Dr. Charles McCutcheon (above) probably used his bicycle for pleasure rather than medical calls. In the 1890s he was superintendent of the Fannie C. Paddock Memorial Hospital in Tacoma, Washington.

switchboard, Dr. William Worrall Mayo had a private line strung between his home and his office above Geisinger and Newton's drugstore. The Rochester *Record and Union* of December 12, 1879, reported:

The telephone line between Dr. Mayo's office and his residence is now up, the machines, or instruments, whichever they are, in position and everything working splendidly. Conversation can be carried on just as rapidly and accurately as though the persons talking were only separated by a few feet instead of a mile.

When the doctor was called out on an especially long trip, he tried to see as many families as he could along the route. The prairie grapevine had a way of preceding him, and families who wanted him to stop hung a signal flag or a colored lantern—which could be seen from the main road—because a three-or-four-mile trek up a ranch trail was wasted time if he wasn't needed. Not all people were that considerate, however. Nothing was more galling to the country doctor than an all-day or all-night ride—usually through inclement weather—to find a false alarm or a lonely hypochondriac at the end. That's when many of them earned their reputations for forthright commentary!

Also involved in the story of medical transportation were the pioneer ambulances. Before special vehicles were developed, the sick, maimed and wounded were hauled by travois, on horseback, in buckboards, ore wagons and prairie schooners. The jostling often finished off what disease or an Indian arrowhead had begun. Just as the Civil War had brought about greater availability and certain advances in medical equipment, it also forced the improvement of medical ambulances. Dr. Jonathan Letterman, who had been a military surgeon on the western frontier before he became medical director of the Army of the Potomac, was particularly instrumental in upgrading the movement and care of the wounded. Following the early engagements of the war, friends and relatives of soldiers searched the battlefields for several days after-

Archives, University of Santa Clara

(Above right) Dr. Frederick C. Gerlach, physician for Santa Clara College, was an early exponent of the motor car. (Below) Dr. Walter Culin was a medical graduate of the University of Pennsylvania who practiced for many years in Coquille, Oregon. He used his boat for business and pleasure trips on the Coquille River. Doctor Culin also had an early Bartlett X-ray machine on which a crank had to be turned to generate electricity.

Mrs. Charles Francis Saunders

wards, and if they were fortunate—carried away those they found in private carriages. By September 17, 1862, when the battle of Antietam was fought, Doctor Letterman had 200 ambulances on the field, and all wounded men were collected within 24 hours.

In the West, however, ambulances didn't become a factor until larger cities developed and hospital care was more acceptable. Then it was not uncommon for the local undertaker to transport both the ailing and the dead—using white horses for the former and black for the deceased.

On a slightly different tack, probably no tale of pioneer medical figures had more of a macabre note than that of Dr. William Keil, founder of a communal Christian colony at Aurora, Oregon, in 1856. A dozen years earlier the Prussian-born doctor-preacher had established a similar settlement at Bethel, Missouri, but when free land became available in the Washington and Oregon Territories, a decision was made to move westward.

No one was more anxious to make the trip than Keil's 19-year-old son, Willie; consequently, Doctor Keil promised him he could lead the caravan. Unfortunately, however, young Willie fell victim to a malaria attack. Not wishing to delay the departure, the doctor ordered an ambulance made out of a light wagon so that Willie could head the party as promised; but four days before departure, the boy died and Doctor Keil was faced with what he considered a moral commitment. From St. Louis he ordered a lead-lined casket which he filled with alcohol. In it he placed the body of his son. The ambulance was converted into a hearse, and Willie led the wagon train all the way to the Pacific where he was finally buried at Enlo, Washington, on the day after Christmas in 1855.

With the turn of the century, Old Dobbin was

Evelyn Hohf Collection

(Above) In South Dakota, Dr. Julius A. Hohf made his calls in an early-day Oakland. (Below) Dr. William W. Mayo was an old-fashioned horse-and-buggy practitioner in Rochester, Minnesota. (Below left) Dr. Charles Mayo, one of his two famous sons, was an advocate of autos as soon as they became practical.

Mayo Clinic

Mayo Clinic

91

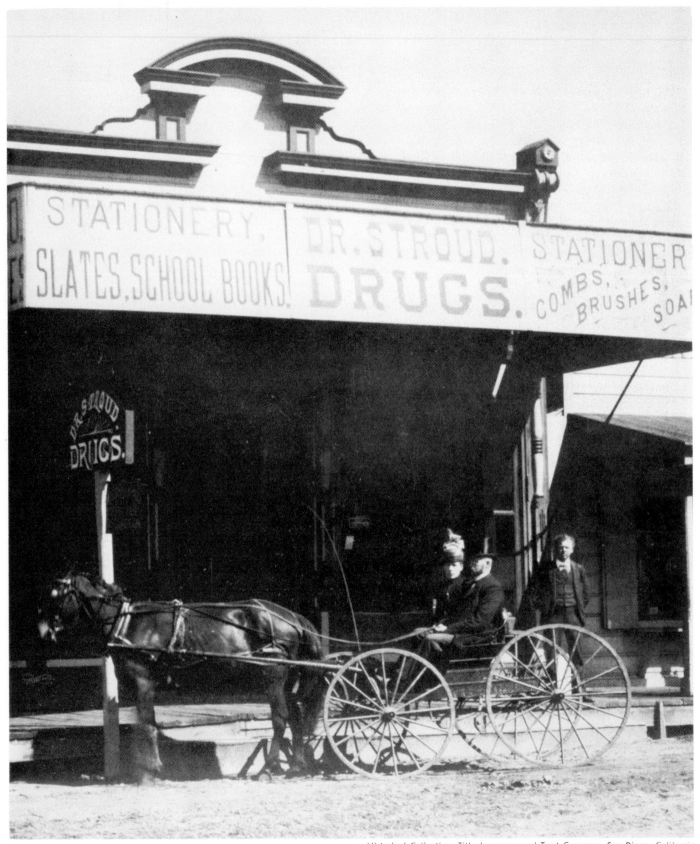

Oceanside, California, residents in 1889 shopped at Dr. Stroud's drugstore and also depended upon the pioneer physician to visit them by horse-and-buggy when they were ill. Doctor-druggists were located in many small towns throughout the West. In the dual role they were able to fare quite well; as one or the other they often had a difficult time making ends meet—particularly if they were poor collectors.

92

(Stimson Collection) Wyoming State Archives and Historical Department

Dr. William W. Crook of Cheyenne, Wyoming, always believed in progress. He had a telephone in his home before there was an exchange in the town, and the first incandescent light in the Wyoming capital city glowed in his parlor. When the horseless carriage became a reality, he was an immediate enthusiast.

(N. H. Rose Collection) Division of Manuscripts, University of Oklahoma Library

Horseless carriages were especially intriguing to doctors, and invariably they were among the first to have a new auto in their town. In the beginning, with no roads to run on, the motor cars didn't help much, but as conditions improved, Old Dobbin began to fade from his medical service role. Doctor Scott of Del Rio, Texas, was obviously pleased with his new Maxwell.

started on his historical journey to oblivion. Sputtering motor cars opened a new chapter in transportation, and invariably doctors were among the first auto owners in nearly every town. Instead of worrying about thrown shoes and livery stable bills, the physicians switched to patching tires and keeping company with a mechanic.

The decade from 1895 to 1905 was a period of unusual mechanical and scientific revolution. The Duryea Motor Wagon Company—the first firm established in America to make gasoline cars—began operation in 1895, the same year Wilhelm Roentgen announced his revolutionary X-ray. Autos and Roentgen machines were soon to change the lives and practices of medical men from Augusta, Maine, to Zillah, Washington.

On the last vestiges of the frontier, a profession which had rendered a century of service via canoe, shank's mare, horseback and buggy began the gradual transition to Stanley Steamers and Winton Runabouts. The country doctor continued to make his rural rounds well past World War I, but much of the romance disappeared when the last saddlebag was retired to the attic.

Montana Historical Society

(Above) In Montana Dr. F. F. Attix made his rounds in a right-hand-drive Franklin. (Below) In Sheridan, Wyoming, Dr. William Frackelton depended upon a Rambler.

Harrah's Automobile Collection

Rambler
MAGAZINE.

PHYSICIAN'S NUMBER

(Opposite page) Dr. Daniel Ream of Siskiyou County, California, was a physician first and a politician second—but sometimes when the county hospital and care of the indigent sick were concerned, he mixed the two together. (Above) Mapping the vast western wilderness was a challenge which attracted Dr. Albert C. Peale away from the practice of medicine. He is shown fourth from the left with a survey team in the Yellowstone region of Wyoming Territory in 1875.

Banker, Lawyer, Political Chief

Before I die I intend to build a city, found a college and become governor of a state....

JOHN EVANS, M.D.

WHILE the pioneer doctor was pursuing his profession on the western frontier, he also participated in a thousand-and-one other endeavors. Probably because his education tended to be better than most of his contemporaries, he was asked to help establish local governments and to become politically involved. Many young physicians went west because of the opportunities the new country offered for wealth and adventure; consequently, their extra-curricular activities sometimes exceeded their medical mission.

Such was the case of Dr. Dorsey Syng Baker, who joined a wagon train on the Oregon Trail in the fall of 1848. On the journey he treated typhoid sufferers, saved a man who had been shot in the abdomen by Indians and generally safeguarded the health of the party. Once in Oregon, he launched an irrepressible career as an entrepreneur. After a fling in the California gold rush country, he established himself at Walla Walla, Washington Territory. The store he opened became an outfitting point for miners flocking to the Clearwater River. He kept so much gold in the store safe that he ultimately went into the banking business. His first sign said simply: "Bank Place." His interests then shifted to livestock and wheat—and, in turn, a way to move those commodities to market. Though partially paralyzed, Doctor Baker plunged into the

Few medical men could match the extra-curricular career of Dr. John Marsh. Teacher, trader, Indian agent, rancher and gold-seeker were among his avocations. He received his license to practice medicine from Mexican authorities in early-day Los Angeles on the strength of his bachelor's degree from Harvard.

PROCLAMATION!

ONE THOUSAND DOLLARS
REWARD.

WHEREAS, Information has been received that a murder was committed on the body of Dr. JOHN MARSH, on the evening of the 24th day of September, ultimo, near Martinez, in the County of Contra Costa, and that one of the persons suspected of said murder, namely, FELIPE MORENA, has eluded arrest and is now at large.

NOW THEREFORE, I, J. NEELY JOHNSON, Governor of the State of California, by virtue of the powers vested in me by law, do hereby offer a reward of One Thousand Dollars for the apprehension of the said Felipe Morena, and his safe delivery into the custody of the Sheriff of Contra Costa County.

WITNESS, my hand, and the Great Seal of State, at Sacramento, this 13th day of October, A. D. 1856.

[SEAL]

J. NEELY JOHNSON.

ATTEST: DAVID F. DOUGLASS,
Secretary of State.

DESCRIPTION:

FELIPE MORENA, commonly called NINO, is a native Californian or Mexican, about 19 or 20 years old; has black hair turning inward at the border ends; complexion dark and cloudy; has a thin beard about the upper lip; has fine white teeth; is about 5½ feet high, of rather slender appearance; weighs about 140 pounds; is of lively and sprightly air and action; speaks Spanish rapidly. His mother resides at San Jose, where it is suspected he may be concealed; if not there, he has probably gone to the southern portion of the State.

The following is a description of the Watch on the person of Dr. Marsh at the time of his murder, and which is supposed to be, or to have been, in the possession of Felipe Morena;

Gold Hunting Detached Lever, marked "Cooper, London," No. 20,038.

When Dr. John Marsh was murdered by three young Mexican ranch hands in a dispute over wages, the above proclamation was issued. Doctor Marsh's intense ambition won him a fortune, but not many friends.

project which became a western legend: the creation of the famed Rawhide Railroad from Walla Walla to the Columbia River. He planned logging operations for ties and trestles, went east to buy rolling stock and battled relentlessly with stockholders and local citizens. Because his motto was "Shun debt as you shun the devil," he practiced economies at every turn. This led to the stories that he ran his trains on wooden rails covered with rawhide strips, which wolves ate and which caused the tracks to warp in the sun. It is generally assumed now that the yarn-spinners over-did it on that phase of Doctor Baker's enterprise—but his grain-filled trains did run, his bank prospered and his Columbia River steamship company made history.

Even more ambitious was "Dr." John Marsh, whose fantastic career extended from coast to coast and finally ended with his murder near Martinez, California, in 1856. Marsh received a bachelor of arts degree from Harvard in 1823. From that point, his storybook life unfolded in dramatic fashion. In Minnesota he tutored the children of Col. Josiah Snelling; read medicine with that State's first physician, Dr. Edward Purcell; served as a mail carrier and Indian agent. He operated a store in Prairie du Chien, Wisconsin, and when he was accused of selling arms to the Indians at the same time he was supposedly negotiating with them for peace, he escaped arrest by plunging farther into the frontier. At Independence, Missouri, he had another store which prospered and then failed. Again he moved on, this time down the Santa Fe Trail where

he was captured by Comanches. Just like in the movies, his life was spared when he doctored up the chief who had an arrowhead imbedded in his arm; after that, Marsh escaped while supposedly looking for medicinal herbs.

Ultimately, he showed up in the tiny pueblo of Los Angeles. Using his bachelor's degree as his only credentials, he convinced the Mexican authorities that he was a physician, and on February 25, 1836, he was officially registered as such. He practiced there for less than a year, taking his fees in cattle hides and tallow. Then he sold out for $500 and headed northward. In the San Joaquin Valley, Don Juan Marchet (as he was

Dr. Charles Jennison of Leavenworth, Kansas, was a Civil War officer and active in the political development of Kansas.

known) bought an extensive land grant and established a ranch at the foot of Mt. Diablo. When the gold rush came, he made a fortune selling cattle and grapes; he even discovered a bonanza himself at "Marsh's Diggings" on the Yuba River. Never a popular man, he was accused of extorting the last pennies from starving settlers as they came across the Sierras and sought aid at his ranch. He built a huge stone house worthy of a wealthy cattle baron, and then, just when he was about to enjoy the fruits of his enterprises, he was murdered by three of his Mexican ranch hands in a dispute over wages.

There were relatively few businesses in which medical doctors didn't become involved. In Arizona Dr. J. G. Barney ran a saloon, Dr. W. H. Bluett operated a lime kiln, Dr. W. S. Sexsmith had a dairy and Dr. J. W. Walters sold "bath closets." In Oregon Dr. Orlando Plummer managed a telegraph line, Dr. William R. Allen supplemented his income by playing his violin at cotillions, and Dr. F. A. Bailey taught school in Scoggins Valley under a contract which permitted him to treat all patients who came to him at the school house. In Montana Dr. Anson Ford owned a lumber yard and Dr. Allan Hardenbrook a sawmill; Dr. George W. Beal was a hotel proprietor; and Dr. Don Lorenzo Byam operated a ferry.

It was that way throughout the Old West. Sometimes it was a matter of ambition, but quite often a doctor had to branch out simply to make a living.

There were doctor-editors, too, notable among them being George L. Miller, a founder of the *Herald* in Omaha, Nebraska, and a dynamic exponent of that city. Dr. Gilbert C. Monell, owner-editor of the *Nebraska Republican,* was one of the three partners in William N. Byers & Co., which founded the *Rocky Mountain News,* though he wasn't present for the historic publishing race in Denver when the first issue of the *News* made it off the press just 20 minutes ahead of the rival *Cherry Creek Pioneer.* Another physician did travel overland with Editor Byers, though. He was Dr. A. F. Peck, who helped finance the journey with part of $300 he found on the body of a horse thief. He had somehow acquired the cadaver after a hanging, probably for furthering his medical education. The first edition of the *News* carried the doctor's professional card:

A. F. PECK, M.D.
Physician and Surgeon
Cache-a-La-Poudre, Nebraska
Where he may at all times be found
when not professionally engaged or
digging gold

Dr. George L. Miller was one of Nebraska's illustrious pioneers. He came to the territory in 1854 as a physician, but he soon found himself in politics. After service in the territorial legislature and as the sutler at Ft. Kearny, he established himself in Omaha where he was one of the founders of the *Herald,* a hard-biting newspaper he edited until 1887.

The University of Nebraska College of Medicine

Dr. Gilbert C. Monell was another physician who was active in early Nebraska journalism. He was a graduate of Union College and practiced in New York before coming west in 1857. He was owner-editor of the *Nebraska Republican* and one of the partners in the company which founded the *Rocky Mountain News* in Denver. He served as first president of the Nebraska State Medical Association in 1868.

The University of Nebraska College of Medicine

Seattle Historical Society

(Parker McAllister painting) The Seattle Times

In the 1850s in Seattle, Washington Territory, Dr. David S. Maynard was, at one and the same time, the town physician, druggist, merchant, superintendent of schools, notary public, justice of the peace, clerk of the court and hospital keeper. He also operated a salmon fishery employing many native tribesmen. During the Indian War of 1855-56, he was sub-agent at the Port Madison Indian Reservation where his friendship with Chief Seattle (depicted in the painting above) was of considerable value. Doctor Maynard was trained by a preceptor and came west with a wagon train in 1850, after a falling out with his first wife. He later married the widow of a cholera victim on that trip. The second Mrs. Maynard (who is pictured below at the doctor's grave) served as his nurse and chief aide in his numerous ventures.

Seattle Historical Society

It was gold which brought many doctors westward. They came to California, Cripple Creek and Alder Gulch, lured by the magic of El Dorado. Dr. Levi J. Russell suggested Auraria (after his hometown in Georgia) as an early name for the city which ultimately became Denver. In Montana Dr. Gaylord G. Bissell was elected judge of the miners' court at Alder Gulch, and when the pro-Confederate argonauts wanted to name the gold camp Varina—for the wife of Jefferson Davis—he refused to sign any of the legal papers. Then he suggested Virginia City, which he said was "southern enough to suit any rebel."

The biographies of scores of pioneer doctors include references to mining endeavors, not all successful. Others prospered indirectly from the gold rushes. In 1853 physicians were involved in two unusual ventures. Dr. Jesse Scott Cunningham bought 4,000 sheep for 75 cents apiece in the Middle West and herded them cross-country to Sacramento. He lost 375 on the way and sold the rest for $11 a head. Dr. Thomas Flint assembled 2,000 sheep and a few other animals in Illinois and drove them successfully through hostile Indians and across the Mojave Desert into California. Pocketing his profits, he stayed to practice at San Juan Bautista where he died in 1904 at the age of 80.

Dr. Brewster M. Higley traveled westward to Kansas to rebuild his life after a losing battle with demon rum and a broken marriage. On the secluded bank of West Beaver Creek in Smith County, Doctor Higley built a tiny cabin and there wrote the words which years later were to become popular as the song "Home on the Range." His original poem is shown above, reprinted in the *Kirwin Chief*, one of two early Kansas newspapers to record it for posterity.

The lure was not always gold, however. Drs. John A. Veatch and W. O. Ayers organized the California Borax Company and in 1864 marketed their initial shipment—12 tons at 39 cents a pound—the first borax produced in America. In 1852 in Seattle (then Oregon Territory) Dr. David Swinson Maynard established the first salmon fishery in the Pacific Northwest; he was also the new town's first physician, first druggist, first justice of the peace, first hospital keeper—and among other things, first to be admitted to the bar.

There were other lawyer-physicians like Dr. Walter Atwood Burleigh of Yankton, Dakota Territory—who also happened to be involved in the steamboating business. And other railroad builders like Dr. William A. Bell of Colorado who founded the Denver & Rio Grande and, on the side, established the Colorado Coal and Iron Company. There were other editors, too, like Dr. Mark F. Hobson, publisher of the weekly

The Kansas State Historical Society

After Dan Kelly, Doctor Higley's violin-playing friend, wrote the original music for "Home on the Range" in the early 1870s, it was played by the Smith Center band.

Jayhawker in Sedgwick, Kansas.

Doctors participated in educational matters, social events, civic affairs, and a few found time for music. Among the latter was Dr. Brewster M. Higley, a prai-

One of the more unusual sidelines of early-day practitioners was that of Dr. "Buffalo Bill" DeVeny. A dead-ringer for William Cody, Doctor DeVeny is said to have represented the "real" Buffalo Bill in various parades and shooting exhibitions. The two look-alikes are shown together below. Though his Wild West show experiences took place mostly in the Middle West, Doctor DeVeny ultimately settled in Portland, Oregon, where he practiced as a foot specialist.

Dr. Hans Lee Pearce

Dr. Hans Lee Pearce

The Kansas State Historical Society

In Smith County, Kansas, the rustic cabin where Dr. Brewster M. Higley wrote the words to "Home on the Range" has been reconstructed and is now a tourist attraction.

rie practitioner who received his medical degree from the State Medical College of Indiana in the spring of 1848. He was an ambitious young man, financing his education by raising tobacco during the summer and chopping wood during the school year. He started his career successfully, first as a demonstrator of anatomy at his alma mater, and then as a country doctor in La-Porte, Indiana. Unfortunately, his wife wasn't able to adjust to her role, and Doctor Higley ultimately turned to the bottle. The marriage failed, his practice suffered and the dejected physician moved westward—to Smith County, Kansas—to try to rebuild his life.

At Gaylord on the Solomon River he practiced among the new settlers and occasionally got out his violin to entertain himself or to enliven a hoe-down. Finally he filed a claim on West Beaver Creek and built a rustic retreat. He spent as much time as he could at his cabin, and as he wandered along the tiny stream, he occasionally watched a buffalo roam . . . or a deer and an antelope play. Then one day he sat down and penned his feeling in a poem he titled "My Western Home." His escape from earlier personal tribulations was pointedly expressed in a line which went "Where seldom is heard a discouraging word. . . ."

Most of the physicians who served with the military in the Old West ultimately doffed their uniforms and went into private practice, often in the vicinity of the frontier posts at which they served. Some continued careers as army doctors, and a small handful pursued a strictly military course, most notable among the latter being Dr. Leonard Wood (shown at left) who, in time, became army chief of staff. This picture was taken when he was a military surgeon in Arizona Territory where he earned the Medal of Honor for gallantry.

Doctor Higley put his verses away, but in time they came to light, and music for them was written by Dan Kelly, one of the doctor's musical cronies. In 1873 the words first appeared in the *Smith County Pioneer*, and on March 21, 1874, in the *Kirwin* (Kans.) *Chief*. Though he little realized it at the time, the frontier physician had created a song—"Home on the Range"—which would live long after he himself was virtually forgotten. Through the years others claimed credit for the original poem, and a legal fight over its source raged more than half a century after Doctor Higley had first committed the words to paper. The old physician, who had found happiness in a second marriage, died in 1909 at the age of 86 and was buried in Shawnee, Oklahoma, never realizing that he had authored a folk-music classic.

Many physicians became mayors of western cities, among them being Dr. Gideon A. Weed, who was twice elected to that office in Seattle, Washington. In addition to his medical practice, Doctor Weed established a pioneer hospital in 1874 and amassed a sizable fortune through real estate transactions.

When President Abraham Lincoln needed a governor appointee for the Dakota Territory, he turned to his family physician, Dr. William Jayne of Springfield, Illinois. Then in his mid-thirties, Doctor Jayne traveled to Yankton, D. T., where he established the government in a log house. He was later elected territorial delegate to congress, after which he returned to Springfield where he was politically, financially and professionally successful.

The Governor Was a Doctor

No extra-curricular activity captivated frontier doctors like the good old American game of politics. They participated in it directly and indirectly, as elected officials and patronage appointees. They represented both major parties, and they were often vocal about their affiliations. Dr. F. A. Bailey of Washington County, Oregon, professed three pet aversions: "quacks, flies and Republicans."

Dr. Calvin Levi Gregory, who moved to Siskiyou County, California, in 1885, reminisced: "When I arrived . . . the county was hopelessly Democratic. After I had lived there two or three years, a lot of us Repub-

105

licans decided to organize and put the Democratic rascals out and put in a lot of Republican rascals."

Doctor Gregory became an arch-foe of his Democratic counterpart, Dr. Daniel Ream (who appears on the jacket of this book). The latter was a typical old-time politician, pulling strings and playing the patronage game to the hilt. The Democratic Party in Siskiyou County was known as "Ream's ring," and he himself was elected coroner, tax collector, sheriff and state senator.

Other pioneer physicians managed to rise higher, however. In several of the western states and territories, men who attained governor's chairs were medical doctors. One of the most noteworthy was Dr. John Evans of Colorado Territory.

A Quaker by birth, Evans studied medicine against his father's will, an early indication of the rebellious individualism which was to mark his illustrious career. When he entered Lynn College in Cincinnati, his angry parent wrote: "Thou art a wayward son of perdition. . . ." Nonetheless, young John won his degree in 1838 and immediately began a somewhat itinerant practice. His journeys took him as far south as New Orleans where he learned about two evils: yellow fever and slavery. As a result of the latter, he became associated with the Underground Railway. In Attica,

(Top left) Dr. John Evans was appointed governor of Colorado Territory in 1862, one of several physicians to be so honored by President Abraham Lincoln. Doctor Evans was one of the founders of Northwestern University, and Evanston, Illinois, was named for him.

(Top right) President U. S. Grant—like Lincoln—also turned to the ranks of medical men to find a governor for Idaho Territory. His choice was Dr. D. W. Ballard, who had been born in Indiana but who came west to Lebanon, Oregon, in 1852. After his term, he and his son operated a drugstore in the Oregon town.

(Bottom left) Dr. James W. Throckmorton was a lawyer-physician who served as the first governor of Texas after the Civil War. He had a short term, however, as he disagreed with General Philip H. Sheridan—who had military control over the state—and was removed from office. He was later a U.S. congressman.

(Bottom right) Other states and territories had doctor-governors, but Texas had a doctor-president. Anson Jones, graduate of Jefferson College in Pennsylvania with a medical degree, went to Texas in 1833 and was the republic's last president before statehood. Jones County and its county seat—Anson—were named in his honor.

Indiana, he established his first regular practice, and when he became appalled at the treatment of the insane in the state, he led a campaign for a hospital of which he was named first superintendent.

As his reputation grew, he was offered a professorship at the Rush Medical College in Chicago, a position he held for eleven years, and it was during that period when he gained national prominence for his demands that Congress declare a quarantine law for cholera which he insisted was contagious. Nothing happened; as usual, he was ahead of his time! In Chicago he acquired wealth through real estate transactions, was instrumental in the construction of the Chicago & Fort Wayne Railroad, helped establish Northwestern University and was named a delegate to the Illinois State Republican convention which endorsed one of his personal friends—Abraham Lincoln—as a candidate for president.

Lincoln's election ultimately resulted in the appointment of Doctor Evans as governor of Colorado Territory in 1862. There he fostered the beef cattle industry, instigated founding of the Colorado Seminary which became the University of Denver, and signed a woman's suffrage law. Only the infamous Sand Creek massacre—the brutal slaughter of some 150 Indians (many of them women and children) by Col. J. M. Chivington's Colorado Volunteers—marred his administration. It was enough, however, to help his detractors force a replacement after President Lincoln was murdered. Doctor Evans elected to remain in Denver where he continued his business pursuits, mostly involved with the building of railroads. He died in that city in 1897 at the age of 83.

Just before President Lincoln appointed Doctor Evans to the Colorado post, he had another governor-

After his term as territorial governor of Colorado, Dr. John Evans remained in Denver where he was particularly active in the building and development of railroad lines. This was his home in the Mile High City.

State Historical Society of Colorado

The Kansas State Historical Society

The first governor of Kansas was Dr. Charles Robinson. His administration was marred by scandal over bond manipulations, but Doctor Robinson himself was acquitted of wrong-doing.

ship to fill in the Dakota Territory. His choice for that position was his family physician in Springfield, Illinois, Dr. William Jayne. A young man in his mid-thirties, Doctor Jayne traveled to Yankton, the territorial capital, in May of 1861 where he established the seat of government in a log house. When he addressed the first legislature, his speech was printed in English, Norwegian, German and French so that the heavily immigrant citizenry would be informed. Instead of completing his term, Governor Jayne was elected territorial delegate to Congress, a position he filled until 1864. He then returned to Springfield, Illinois, to resume his practice. He also served four terms as mayor of that city and was a state senator.

In Arizona Dr. Lewis S. Owings, a mining developer from Mesilla, was elected governor of the short-lived Provisional Government of the Territory of Arizona in 1860. Later he became the first mayor of Denison, Texas. The Territory of New Mexico was headed by two physicians, William Carr Lane and Henry Connelly. Dr. D. W. Ballard, a farmer-doctor from Lebanon, Oregon, was appointed governor of Idaho Territory by President Ulysses S. Grant.

The history of Texas is highlighted by medical men in political roles. Among them was Dr. Anson Jones, last president of the republic, elected in 1844. Dr. Ashbel Smith was the first minister to England and France and the first surgeon general of the Republic of Texas.

Dr. Amos Walker Barber was named secretary of state in Wyoming's first statehood election in 1890. Soon afterwards, Governor Francis E. Warren resigned to become senator, and Doctor Barber automatically assumed the governorship in an acting capacity. He served for two years, but the emotionally-charged Johnson County Range War during his administration helped lead to his defeat in a special election to fill the final two years of Warren's term.

After the Civil War Dr. James W. Throckmorton was elected governor of the state. However, the problems of reconstruction resulted in federal military control, and when Governor Throckmorton—who had been a Confederate general—couldn't agree on policy with General Philip H. Sheridan, commander of the district, the doctor was removed and a new governor appointed.

The first governor of Kansas was also a physician. Dr. Charles Robinson came to the area in 1854 and was a rabid participant in the free-soil movement. When the so-called Kansas Free-State legislature met in Topeka in 1856 to approve a constitution, he was introduced as governor. Congress didn't approve of this premature action, however, and Doctor Robinson

was thwarted until the state was properly admitted in 1861, at which time he was elected its first official leader. His administration was shaken by impeachment proceedings against him and other officials over a question of bond manipulation. Doctor Robinson was acquitted.

Wyoming had back-to-back doctor-governors in its early years of statehood. The first was Amos W. Barber, who had been elected secretary of state in 1890 but who assumed the governor's chair in an acting capacity when his predecessor—Francis E. Warren—became U. S. senator. Doctor Barber's administration suffered through the much-publicized Johnson County War, and when an election was held to fill the final

Wyoming's third governor—John E. Osborne—was involved in a rather grisly episode in western medical history, if the legend of "Big Nose" George Parrott is reasonably accurate.

Parrott was leader of a gang of outlaws which terrorized frontier towns in Wyoming and neighboring territories during the 1870s. In time, the notorious bandit was captured and returned to Rawlins. Then, when he assaulted a jailer in a desperate attempt to escape, an infuriated mob broke into the hoosegow and strung him up on the nearest telegraph pole.

Supposedly, the "official medical witness" at the unofficial necktie party was Doctor Osborne, who was given the body for whatever use he cared to make of it. Local lore has it that he preserved the cadaver in a strong salt solution for occasional dissection and study. It is also said that he trimmed a medical kit with skin from Parrott's chest and a pair of two-tone shoes from the late outlaw's thighs. As a final gesture, the doctor sawed off the top of Big Nose's skull and presented it to Dr. Lillian Heath, who reportedly used it for a door-stop.

In 1955 the *Rocky Mountain News* announced that the remainder of Parrott's long-lost body was discovered in a whiskey barrel during excavations for a construction project. The story added that the unique door-stop—on display at the Union Pacific Museum in Omaha—fit what was left of the skull perfectly!

Wyoming State Archives and Historical Department

two years of Governor Warren's term, Dr. John E. Osborne, a Democrat, was the winner. The bitterness engendered by the range conflict caused Doctor Osborne to attempt a dramatic—but unsuccessful—assumption of office. Early in December of 1892, in the dark of night, he crawled through a window of the governor's office with some blankets and slept there until morning. The next day he demanded the state seal and the keys to the office from Acting Governor (also Secretary of State) Barber. Doctor Barber held firm, however, and Doctor Osborne had to wait for the constitutional "first Monday in January" to be sworn into office.

Throughout the Old West other physicians plunged into the political wars. There were dozens of M.D. mayors like Dr. Gideon A. Weed of Seattle, Washington. There were scores of aldermen, commissioners and supervisors like Dr. Richard Beverly Cole of San Francisco. Doctor Cole was elected in spite of his ability to get involved in most unpolitical controversies. When James King of William, editor of the *Daily Eve-*

ning Bulletin was gunned down in 1856, Doctor Cole publicly accused fellow physicians of leaving a sponge in the wound, thus killing the newspaperman whose caustic editorials had aroused bitter enmities. On another occasion, Doctor Cole delivered a paper before the California Medical Society entitled "Obstetrics and Diseases of Women." That sounded harmless enough, but in his text, he blandly proclaimed that three out of four California women were no longer virgins by the time they were 15, and in "yielding to the solicitations of the opposite sex" they made themselves prey to disease. All hell broke loose! Doctor Cole was castigated from coast to coast, and in California his sizable practice—especially the women patients—dwindled away. In time he regained his professional reputation, but he always bore the scars of his verbal forthrightness.

Doctors of politics often had tongues as sharp as their scalpels, and the bitter pills they dished out were not always medicinal. In the process they contributed immensely to the development of the frontier.

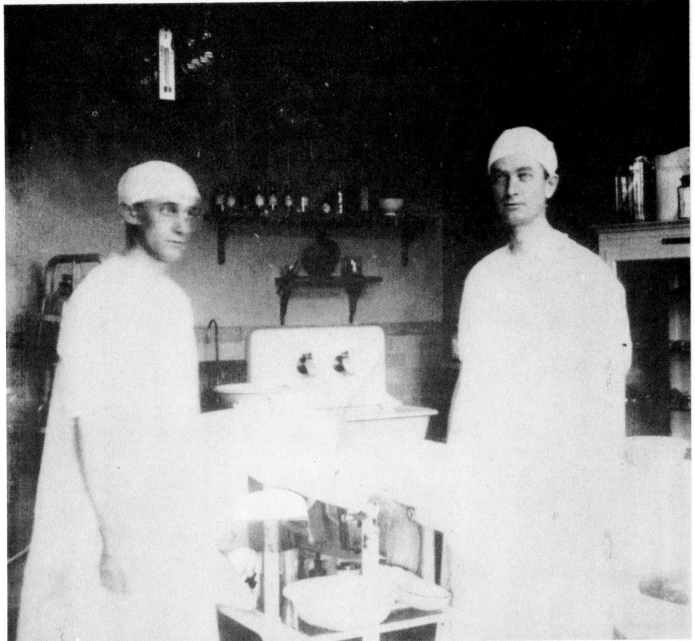

(Opposite page) Some of the West's earliest hospitals were started by physicians right in their own homes. A little more elaborate than some was Dr. James Raizon's sanitarium in Trinidad, Colorado. He and his family lived in one side of the building, while patients were cared for in the other. (Above) Few names in western medical history are as well known as those of the Mayo brothers, Drs. William J. and Charles H. They are shown here preparing for surgery at St. Mary's Hospital, which they and their father—Dr. William Worrall Mayo—were instrumental in establishing in Rochester, Minnesota.

From the Pest House: Nowhere But Up

The cause of suffering humanity knows no religion and no sex.

MOTHER ALFRED
St. Mary's Hospital
Rochester, Minnesota

Except for a few rugged outdoorsmen, doctors were not particularly pleased with their long hours of confinement in a saddle or on a hard buggy seat. Consequently, they jumped at a chance to reduce their country mileage whenever possible. So much of it was actually wasted time—time which could be better spent reading the professional journals which were beginning to appear with more regularity, or to organize a sanitation committee to get the hogs and garbage out of the streets.

Hospitals were not well thought of during most of the 19th century. They were places where people went to die—or they were institutions for paupers or the homeless who had no one to care for them. Public "pest houses" were established for contagious diseases, and these didn't help improve the general attitude. The example of the latter shown here was known as the Dale Street Infirmary in St. Paul, Minnesota.

The staff of the St. Paul "pest house" (shown on the opposite page) did not exude any feeling of warmth, kindness and loving care. Pest houses were places of confinement, and medical attention was often secondary. The reputations of such institutions were detrimental to pioneer hospitals until the public began to recognize the difference.

The best way, of course, was to bring the patients to them—or to get as many sick people congregated as possible so they could all be visited on a single trip. The obvious answer was a hospital of some kind.

In the 1800s, though, hospitals—the few that existed —were not popular. They were, in the minds of most people, places to go to die, not to get well. In addition, they bore the stigma of prison, pauperism and pest houses. The indigent and homeless might be interested in hospitals—but not folks with families.

They had heard about medieval hospitals where

In the same bed lay individuals affected with infectious diseases besides others only slightly unwell; on the same couch, body against body, a woman groaned in the pangs of labor, a nursing infant writhed in convulsions, a typhus patient burned in the delirium of fever, a consumptive coughed his hollow cough. . . . The whole building fairly swarmed with the most horrible vermin, and the air of morning was so vile in the sick wards that the attendants did not venture to enter

them without a sponge saturated with vinegar held before their faces.   (Max Nordau)

Needless to say, the hospital concept had to be "sold" to a skeptical public—and sometimes it took years for an institution to prove itself. Doctors had to convince doubting patients and their relatives that odds for surgical success were far greater where proper facilities were available. Emergency operations performed on a kitchen table, a parlor sofa (after the cats had been chased off) or an unbolted door thrown over two sawhorses were not conducive to high recovery rates.

Into the face of this general hostile attitude, doctors, laymen and religious leaders moved to build refuges for the sick. Often these were emergency measures, like Dr. Pedro Prat's crude canvas-and-driftwood hospital on the shores of San Diego Bay in 1769. The early missions in California and throughout the Southwest provided care for the sick and injured. Dr. Frederico

Zervan was physician in charge of the military infirmary in the Alamo at San Antonio in 1805. At Fort Vancouver on the Columbia River, Dr. Meredith Gairdner established a hospital in 1833 where he treated more than 200 victims of intermittent fever. At Waiilatpu a few years later, missionary-physician Marcus Whitman cared for ailing travelers on the Oregon Trail, using part of his main building as a hospital during a measles epidemic in 1847. Military forts usually had some form of hospital or infirmary where both soldiers and civilians were treated.

At first men were in the vast majority on the frontier. They were adventurous, transient individuals who thought little about medical attention. They were young and vigorous, with visions of great wealth to be found in the gold country; a hospital was the last thought in their mind.

But the wilderness was rugged; disease and privation took a heavy toll; so did the excesses of alcohol and other pleasures. Even worse, the riches of El Dorado seldom matched the dreams of the argonauts, and when sickness befell them, they often had nowhere to turn. They became the paupers and destitute of the new country, and, in most cases, local governments assumed the responsibility for their care.

Generally, then, hospitals in the Old West got started somewhat as they existed in "the States" and in Europe. Depending upon the locale and the circum-

(Above) The men's ward at Ancker Hospital in St. Paul, Minnesota, was a barracks-like affair. Note the window weights being used for traction. (Below) Episcopal Bishop Daniel S. Tuttle established St. Mark's Hospital in Salt Lake City, Utah, in 1872. The first location was a rented adobe house.

stances, they were the poor farms and almshouses established by county commissioners and city councils to help the indigent. Where contagious diseases were involved, they became "pest houses"—and from that lowly beginning, there was no way to go but up.

These predecessors of hospitals got started in many ways. In some cases, public officials would appeal to a local doctor to make a place in his own home for a pauper, at government expense. In many areas Catholic nuns were given contracts to care for the penniless sick. In some towns, ladies' committees—often representing Protestant denominations or Masonic lodges—established the first infirmaries for the poor. No matter who did it, though, funds and facilities usually were limited, and the paupers were anything but pampered.

(Right) Good Samaritan Hospital in Portland, Oregon, was completed in 1875. The University of Oregon Medical School's first location was in a pasture behind it. (Below) The Mayo brothers—Doctors Will and Charlie, as they were known—operated at St. Mary's Hospital, Rochester, Minnesota, before an intense group of observers.

(Above) Northwest Medicine, "100 Years of Medical Education in Oregon"

(Below) St. Mary's Hospital, Rochester, Minnesota

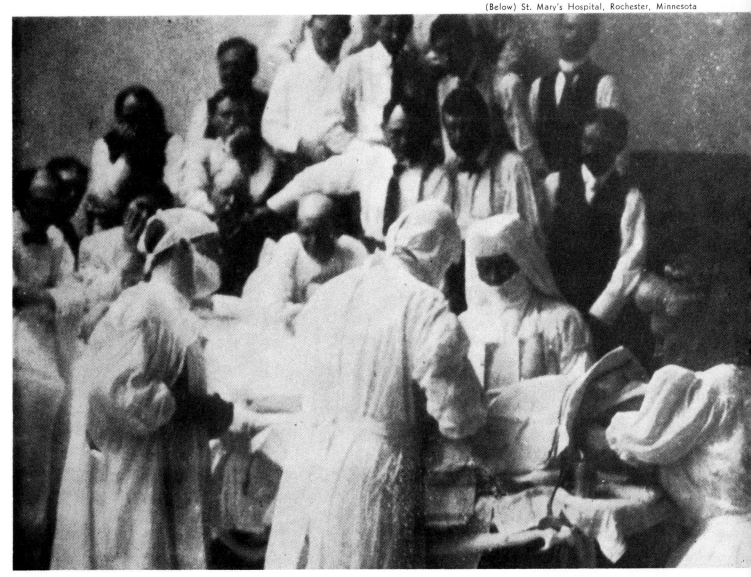

The so-called county hospitals were particularly bad. Usually they were established in an old farmhouse, a run-down hotel or some other second-rate building. Because contracts were awarded to the lowest bidders, penury was the order of the day—and, of course, the patients got the hind-most. Doctors were often paid in "shin plasters," as county scrip was called. Grand juries were continually investigating scandals and fees; frontier newspaper editors seemed to take particular delight in lambasting hospital administration. In San Francisco in 1871 a jury recommended that surgery should be practiced in a special room, not in the wards where all patients could watch. In Arizona in 1883 the Sisters of St. Joseph were challenged on the grounds that a dollar a day was too much to charge for housing the ailing poor. In Yreka, California, Dr. Daniel Ream was accused in 1872 of keeping indigent patients unnecessarily long in the county hospital of which he was administrator by dint of political patronage. In 1889 the nuns at the new St. Mary's Hospital in Rochester, Minnesota, were castigated by bigots for including a chapel "for the exercises of popery."

But there were bright spots, too.

On April 6, 1858, the Vancouver Ladies of Charity— Catholics, Protestants and Jews—held their first meet-

(Right) Railroad companies often established special hospitals for the employees, though sometimes a small monthly fee was deducted from paychecks. This was the Northern Pacific's Stampede Tunnel infirmary. (Below) St. Mary's Sanitarium, established at Muskogee, Indian Territory, by Dr. F. B. Fite, is reported to be the first hospital in what is now Oklahoma.

ing in Washington Territory. They were concerned about a young consumptive in the settlement who had no one to care for him, so they turned to the Sisters of Charity of Providence—five pioneer nuns who had traveled 6,000 miles to assist the Jesuit missionaries in the Pacific Northwest. Mother Joseph, an indomitable woman who was to play a leading role in numerous

Northern Pacific Railway

early hospitals, agreed to provide part of a 16 × 20 frame structure which she had intended to use as a laundry and bakery. Members of the ladies' society (who contributed 12½ cents a week in dues) covered the rough wall boards with paper, installed four beds and St. Joseph Hospital became a reality. The tubercular John Lloyd, for whom the project was begun, be-

came the first patient. Within two months he was dead, but the hospital became a permanent institution.

Another dedicated group of women organized the Ladies Benevolent Home in Wichita, Kansas, in 1885. Two years later "and Hospital" was added to its title as both homeless and sick were cared for. To help pay the way, however, rooms were often rented to travel-

ing salesmen who preferred the hospital to the local hotels. In Walthill, Nebraska, Dr. Susan La Flesche Picotte—an Indian woman born in a tepee on a reservation and later a graduate of the Philadelphia Women's Medical School—agitated, pleaded and begged for five years to raise funds for a small hospital. Then she continued to agitate, plead and beg to get the Indians to use the new facility.

In Portland, Oregon, Bishop W. Morris, an Episcopalian, preached a sermon on March 8, 1874, during which he said: "It is time that the Protestants, as well as others, were engaged in the eminently Christian work of caring for the sick." Whereupon he opened a fund drive for the Good Samaritan Hospital. Historians relate that his approach was a strategic one, because in Portland—as in other areas of the West—many Protestants were inclined to be jealous because of Catholic dominance in the field. By October of 1875 his hospital was ready for service. After three successful years of operation, the institution almost succumbed—because the roads leading to it were so bad that physicians couldn't convey their patients "over ruts of unknown depth." Fortunately, Bishop Morris resisted the temptation to sell the building, a new road

(Above) On the Seattle, Washington, waterfront, Dr. Alex de Soto—a physician with missionary zeal—converted an old coastal steamer, the *Idaho*, into his Wayside Mission Hospital. It was a charitable institution for down-and-outers. (Below) The unusual ship hospital had its own pharmacy. Doctor de Soto's office was in the pilot house.

(Ruth Herold) Department of Biomedical History, University of Washington School of Medicine

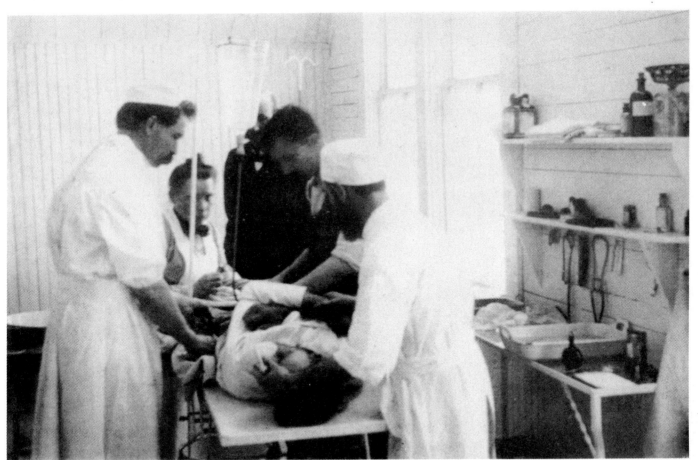

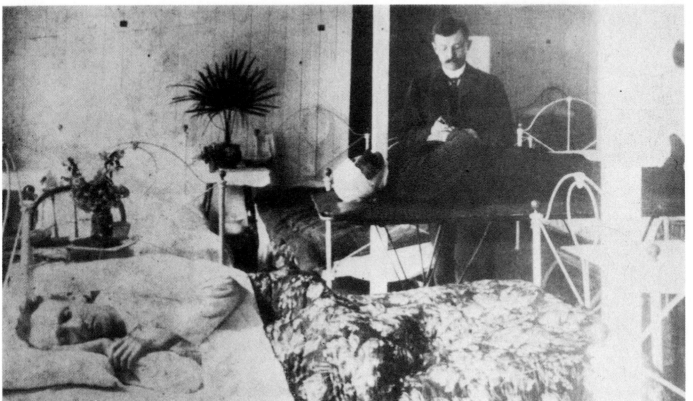

(Top) The Wayside Mission Hospital had its own small surgery. Dr. Alex de Soto, the benevolent physician, who fed and treated thousands of waterfront indigents, stood at the patient's head. (Bottom) Patients were accommodated in the *Idaho's* staterooms. Dope addicts received special attention at Doctor de Soto's mission in "applied Christianity."

(Top) St. Luke's Hospital, which opened in Denver in 1886, had its own tiny lake. The dirt road in front had a tendency to become a quagmire when rains came. (Bottom) In Bisbee, Arizona Territory, Dr. Thomas Darlington persuaded mine officials to erect the first Copper Queen Hospital in 1884. Railroad, mining and logging companies were responsible for a number of early-day infirmaries, some of which became permanent institutions.

Northern Pacific Railway

In 1884 the Northern Pacific Hospital at Missoula, Montana, was completed at a cost of approximately $14,000, with an employee beneficial association spearheading the project. It was destroyed by fire in 1892, at which time Dr. John J. Buckley, the chief surgeon, moved his office to a boxcar. A new building was erected the following year.

was built and "an alarming indebtedness of $636" was cleared up. In 1887 a small wooden building was erected on the hospital grounds, and the newly formed University of Oregon Medical School began operation, using the Good Samaritan Hospital for most of its classes and clinical demonstrations.

Money was a continual problem for the pioneer hospitals. When towns developed and "ladies' aid societies" were formed, quilting bees, ice cream socials,

concerts and innumerable other activities were held to raise sorely needed funds. Before that, though, the Catholic sisters—in almost every territory and state in which they worked—were forced to go on begging missions. They also prayed for miracles.

In Omaha, Nebraska, in 1870, two hospitals had been built and two had burned down (an all too common occurrence) when five Sisters of Mercy stepped off the gangplank of a Missouri River steamboat. They

(Left) The Denver General Hospital in 1897 featured gas lights and a well-scrubbed look, a great improvement over the vermin-ridden almshouses of the past. (Right) The mining town of Robinson, Utah (no longer in existence) boasted the Tintic Hospital. The quest for gold and other metals took a heavy toll in dead and injured, so medical facilities were much appreciated by the miners.

State Historical Society of Colorado   Utah State Historical Society

started to teach school, but the need for a hospital was so great—particularly for those injured on the railroad—that two of the sisters set out to visit camps and towns along the Union Pacific line in quest of funds. It was a miracle, they thought, when $10,000 was contributed. But their contractor undid it by sadly underestimating construction costs, and they needed help again. Their prayers produced James M. Pattee, the famed "Lottery King" who came to Omaha that same year and formed a partnership with Dr. J. W. B. Gardiner, who was on the hospital staff. In 1871 Pattee advertised a "$150,000 Grand Gift Concert in Aid of the Mercy Hospital" scheduled for the Redick Opera House, first prize being the opera house itself. Like all Pattee schemes, though, all major prizes were won by shills or nonexisting individuals—but the good sisters didn't know this, and the $8,100 he contributed to them was their second miracle as far as they were concerned.

Meanwhile, other hospitals were being built throughout the West. In the mining camps and railroad towns an early version of pre-paid medical care helped provide the funds. Typical was St. Mary's in

(Above) In Dodge City, Kansas, Dr. T. L. McCarty converted this former hotel into a hospital. (Below) In Seattle, Washington, the Sisters of Charity of Providence cared for ailing paupers at the county "poor farm" as early as 1877. The next year they converted an old city residence into a hospital of their own. Before the building pictured below was begun in 1882, the sister superior once carried the total cash assets of Providence Hospital—25 cents—in her purse.

(Above) The Northwestern Hospital for Women and Children in Minneapolis featured a diet kitchen. There was a time when hospital patients in earlier institutions were lucky to get something to eat. (Below) The Santa Clara (Calif.) County Hospital was given a palatial look by a pioneer artist. Brother physicians—Drs. Benjamin and Andrew Jackson Cory—were instrumental in its construction in 1875.

Tucson, Arizona, where the Southern Pacific Railroad deducted 50 cents a month from the wages of its employees which went to the hospital. In Philipsburg, Montana, Dr. William H. Allen opened a private subscription hospital in 1886, charging subscribers $1.25 a month when well and free service when sick.

Much earlier, as the first flush of the California gold rush wore off, many alien argonauts concentrated in San Francisco. Among them were numerous Frenchmen who formed a benevolent society on December 28, 1851. A hospital was the group's major goal, and dues of one dollar a month were assessed members for which full care was given. Within a year the French Hospital—which other national societies were to copy—was in successful operation.

Other hospitals appeared in a variety of quarters. Dr. Thomas Maghee opened a small one in a wing of the Rawlins, Wyoming, jail. In Missoula, Montana, when

the Northern Pacific Hospital burned in 1892, Dr. John J. Buckley shifted operations to a boxcar. In Sacramento, California, a private hospital in "a miserable canvas building" was washed away in the flood in 1850. St. Mary's Hospital in Virginia City, Montana, was established in a log building which had earlier been a primitive courthouse. In Seattle, Washington, Dr. Alex de Soto, a missionary-physician who claimed to have overcome the morphine habit through faith, converted an old steamboat, the *Idaho*, into his Wayside Mission Hospital.

During the 19th century hundreds of hospitals were founded, and each, of course, had its individual story. Some succeeded and lived on; others languished and died. They collected cash if they could, gave free service when needed or they accepted public contribu-

(Left) The first medical school in Minneapolis was established in the Winslow House taken over by the Minnesota College Hospital in the mid-1880s. (Right) Pioneer hospitals were always strapped for funds. Even lotteries were used to raise construction money. This particular one in Lincoln, Nebraska, appeared to have all the necessary official blessing.

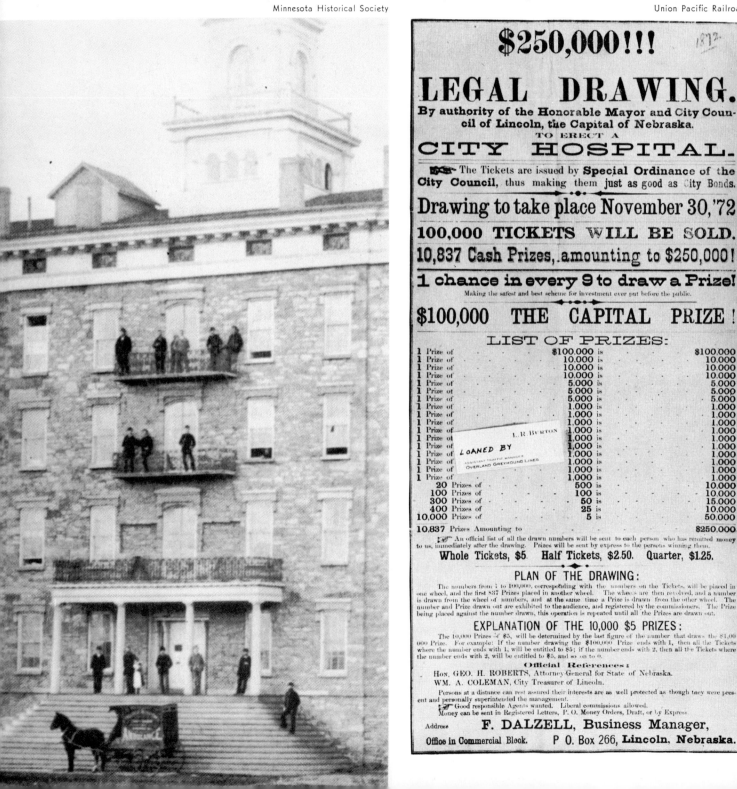

1872.

$250,000!!!

LEGAL DRAWING.

By authority of the Honorable Mayor and City Council of Lincoln, the Capital of Nebraska.

TO ERECT A

CITY HOSPITAL.

☞ The Tickets are issued by **Special Ordinance of the City Council**, thus making them just as good as City Bonds.

Drawing to take place November 30, '72

100,000 TICKETS WILL BE SOLD.

10,837 Cash Prizes, amounting to $250,000!

1 chance in every 9 to draw a Prize!

Making the safest and best scheme for investment ever put before the public.

$100,000 THE CAPITAL PRIZE!

LIST OF PRIZES:

1 Prize of	$100,000 is	$100,000
1 Prize of	10,000 is	10,000
1 Prize of	10,000 is	10,000
1 Prize of	10,000 is	10,000
1 Prize of	5,000 is	5,000
1 Prize of	5,000 is	5,000
1 Prize of	5,000 is	5,000
1 Prize of	1,000 is	1,000
1 Prize of	1,000 is	1,000
1 Prize of	1,000 is	1,000
1 Prize of	1,000 is	1,000
1 Prize of	1,000 is	1,000
1 Prize of	1,000 is	1,000
1 Prize of	1,000 is	1,000
1 Prize of	1,000 is	1,000
1 Prize of	1,000 is	1,000
20 Prizes of	500 is	10,000
100 Prizes of	100 is	10,000
300 Prizes of	50 is	15,000
400 Prizes of	25 is	10,000
10,000 Prizes of	5 is	50,000

10,837 Prizes Amounting to $250,000

☞ An official list of all the drawn numbers will be sent to each person who has remitted money to us, immediately after the drawing. Prizes will be sent by express to the persons winning them.

Whole Tickets, $5.   Half Tickets, $2.50.   Quarter, $1.25.

PLAN OF THE DRAWING:

The numbers from 1 to 100,000, corresponding with the numbers on the Tickets, will be placed in one wheel, and the first 837 Prizes placed in another wheel. The wheels are then revolved, and a number is drawn from the wheel of numbers, and at the same time a Prize is drawn from the other wheel. The number and Prize drawn out are exhibited to the audience, and registered by the commissioners. The Prize being placed against the number drawn, this operation is repeated until all the Prizes are drawn out.

EXPLANATION OF THE 10,000 $5 PRIZES:

The 10,000 Prizes of $5, will be determined by the last figure of the number that draws the $100,000 Prize. For example: If the number drawing the $100,000 Prize ends with 1, then all the Tickets where the number ends with 1, will be entitled to $5; if the number ends with 2, then all the Tickets where the number ends with 2, will be entitled to $5, and so on to 0.

Official References:

Hon. GEO. H. ROBERTS, Attorney-General for State of Nebraska.

WM. A. COLEMAN, City Treasurer of Lincoln.

Persons at a distance can rest assured their interests are as well protected as though they were present and personally superintended the management.

☞ Good responsible Agents wanted. Liberal commissions allowed.

Money can be sent in Registered Letters, P. O. Money Orders, Draft, or by Express.

Address   F. DALZELL, Business Manager,

Office in Commercial Block.   P. O. Box 266, **Lincoln, Nebraska.**

L. R. BURTON

LOANED BY
ASSISTANT TRAFFIC MANAGER
OVERLAND GREYHOUND LINES

tions and gifts. In 1890, for instance, Fannie C. Paddock Memorial Hospital of Tacoma, Washington, acknowledged donations of "1 barrel of flour, 1 case of claret, 1 tub butter, 1 case coal oil, 2 bottles of wine, 1 tub apple butter, 5 gallons port wine, 1 dozen gallons of whiskey and 50 pounds of granulated sugar." At the Wayside Mission Hospital, Doctor de Soto's patients fished driftwood out of Puget Sound which was dried and cut up to heat his unusual infirmary.

Special hospitals were established for the insane, many of which started under conditions comparable to the miserable pest houses of the period. Tuberculars were treated in sanitariums, some of which were opened by physicians as private ventures. Mineral springs, which had been used by the Indians for curative purposes, became the sites of hydropathic hos-

(Above) Health spas were extremely popular in the Old West. Navajo Soda Springs at Manitou, Colorado, attracted these visitors in the 1870s. (Below) Dr. Andrew Jackson Hunter's Hot Springs Hotel was a mecca for the ailing in Montana.

Riley County (Kans.) Historical Museum

Denver Public Library Western Collection

pitals and health spas.

It was popular in the late 1800s to visit these latter institutions, to bathe in and drink of the generally distasteful waters. It was also highly profitable for entrepreneurs like Dr. William Abraham Bell, a British-born physician who came to the Rocky Mountains with a railroad survey party and stayed to develop a resort at Colorado's Manitou Springs. Or Dr. Andrew J. Hunter, who was attracted to Montana by the gold rush in 1864, but who found a greater bonanza at Hunter's Hot Springs in present Park County where he built a large hotel and bath house before selling out in

(Above left) Medicinal waters were widely advertised as cure-alls. (Above right) Another popular attraction at Manitou Springs, Colorado, was Little Chief Iron Springs. (Below) Private promoters and railroad companies developed and publicized elaborate health resorts. In New Mexico, Montezuma Hot Springs offered curative baths to sufferers of a long list of afflictions.

Denver Public Library Western Collection

(Above) Health caves of dubious worth were also promoted as natural avenues to health. The sulphur vapors of Glenwood Springs, Colorado, depicted here did not help J. H. (Doc) Holliday, the notorious Old West gambler, who tried them just before his death in 1887. (Below) This advertisement appeared in a Hailey, Idaho, newspaper on June 5, 1886.

1885. In effect, the rich were soaked two ways!

From their scant and sometimes scandalous beginnings, many hospitals on the western frontier survived and developed into outstanding permanent institutions. Gradually they overcame the reticence of the pioneers who believed that a man's home is his castle, and that's where he should live and die—not in some strange building among people he didn't even know. Maybe that's the way George C. Coffee felt when he entered St. Joseph Hospital in Vancouver, Washington Territory. The final billing on his account indicated that if he had to go—without friends or family to comfort him—at least he should have "one for the road:"

110 days attendance	$110.00
2 bottles brandy and	
6 bottles whiskey	8.00
Burial expenses	25.00

(Opposite page) The J. P. Jelinek Drugstore of St. Paul, Minnesota, was typical of pre-1900 pharmacies. Shelves and counters were full of patent medicines, including Jelinek's own Corn Cure. (Above) Like many physicians, Dr. James Raizon of Trinidad, Colorado, also ran his own drugstore. It gave him a second source of income, a ready supply of medicines and a base of operations. The spittoon by the stove was a sanitary necessity of the era.

Leeches, Laudanum and Soda Water

Wonderful little our fathers knew.
Half of their remedies cured you dead—

RUDYARD KIPLING
Our Fathers of Old

THE drugstore was the pioneer doctor's arsenal, the druggist his alter ego. It was not uncommon for the local physician to be the pharmacist, too—and in some communities it was the other way around.

Invariably, the man who dispensed tinctures in the town's medical emporium was called "Doc," and—whether he was a physician or not—he became involved in diagnoses, treatments and even minor sur-

gery. Often this was true because of the unavailability of regular doctors.

In some places the drugstore was the hangout for the town loafers. There were benches around the pot-bellied stove and large spittoons or sand boxes for the tobacco-chewers. Because of the setting, conversations sometimes tended toward the aches and ills of local residents. This was especially true when someone would come in with a personal complaint, and "Doc" would say, "Stick out your tongue"—right in front of a curious audience.

In the early days, drugs did not come in a ready-to-

use state. From the supply houses in the larger cities, the frontier apothecaries received bulk shipments of roots, herbs, leaves, bark and other natural or partially-processed materials. Using these basic elements, the druggists mashed and pounded with mortar and pestle —or used drug mills like old-fashioned coffee grinders —until the desired results were achieved. They mixed solutions, compounded strange-smelling formulae and measured powder doses which were packaged in tiny squares of paper. Some pharmacists had pill-making machines and suppository molds for special requirements. Most of them kept a ready supply of hungry,

(Left) The Central Drugstore was a corner hangout in Leavenworth, Kansas, in the 1860s. In addition to a full stock of medicines, it also featured Raspberry Lemonade Essence, made right in the back shop. (Below) In the 19th century, druggists concocted prescriptions from bulk products, pulverizing them with mortar and pestle. Unusual hand-blown glass bottles— which were to become collectors' items—contained the necessary ingredients for frontier medicine.

The mining camps of the Old West had an itinerant quality. When gold was found somewhere else, once-prosperous towns disappeared almost overnight. In California an imaginative pharmacist named Justin Gates decided that a mobile drugstore was the best way to keep up with his wandering customers. His pharmacy-on-wheels became a welcome sight to argonauts and the pioneer physicians practicing among them.

Other druggists settled in tiny towns in the mountains and on the prairies, hopeful that enough people would file a claim nearby so they'd have someone to sell to. The small store below —in Dorrance, Kansas—typified the business optimism of the frontier pharmacists.

℞

Parke, Davis & Company

blood-sucking leeches for the doctors who favored that form of treatment.

Nostalgically, the vintage drugstores are remembered for the myriad bottles and jars of ornate design and varied hues which were to become prized collec-

tors' items of future generations. Almost every store, too, had its show globes, gaudy carboys filled with bright, colored liquids which served as a professional trademark. Occasionally, glass jars containing pickled tape worms, gall stones and other less appealing sub-

The Kansas State Historical Society

stances were displayed; at least they provided conversation pieces for the hangers-on.

From the beginning, most Old West drugstores carried an endless variety of merchandise. Kerosene, school supplies, cigars, soda water, licorice sticks and whiskey—medicinal or otherwise—were all available.

At the turn of the century when the new-fangled horseless carriages began to make their appearance, some druggists went into the gasoline-selling business —using a five-gallon container with a potato jammed on the spout.

Whether physicians operated them or not, drug-

(Above) Dodge City, Kansas, raucous cowtown where Wyatt Earp was once marshal and Bat Masterson, the sheriff, probably needed a drugstore more than most places. Doctors were constantly patching up gunshot victims and the other results of cowboy revelry, so they needed plenty of supplies. The photograph reproduced here was taken at the City Drug Store in 1887.

(Below) Mills & Purdy's Excelsior Drugstore in Yankton, Dakota Territory, was captured on film in 1870 by Stanley J. Morrow, itinerant photographer of the era. The store, which also sold groceries, was a popular corner hangout for pioneer residents of the Missouri River town. Old-time pharmacies had a natural attraction for loafers, a characteristic which later druggists capitalized upon by installing soda fountains.

A prominent mortar and pestle advertised Parchen and Paynter's City Drug Store in Helena, Montana, in 1872 when this picture was taken. Show globes (seen in the store window) were also widely recognized trademarks of pioneer pharmacies. The ornamental carboys filled with bright-colored liquids supposedly date back to the alchemists of the 16th century—but their exact origin has been a controversial subject for drug historians.

133

stores were often used as a clearing house for sick calls in the days before telephones. They provided a strategic message center when a doctor was away from his office, because unless he practiced out of his own home and had a wife or housekeeper to receive callers, he was virtually incommunicado on his rounds. The idea of a medical receptionist was unheard of.

Because of the demand—and because they were profitable—patent medicines crammed the drugstore shelves. They were nicely packaged, extremely well advertised and carried easy-to-follow instructions so that every semi-literate person could (he thought) become his own doctor. Even the physician-pharmacists were guilty of pushing the worthless nostrums.

Mostly, though, the druggists stayed busy enough concocting legitimate prescriptions for the doctors in their area—if they could decipher the Latin and the hand-writing. Not all the remedies were included in the pharmacopoeia; sometimes the physicians—especially the eclectics who tried a little of everything—would order mixtures of their own creation or even variations of the local "granny" medicines. Every area

The soda fountain became a drugstore institution in the latter part of the 1800s. It was a better attraction, provided more income and was less messy than a pot-bellied stove and a sand box. A lime phosphate might be dawdled over, but an old-time loafer could make a single chaw last all day. (Below) The back-bar of the Moritz drugstore in Denver was a veritable high altar.

(Top) Drugstores—like doctors' offices—turned up in every imaginable kind of structure on the frontier. In Coulson, Montana (predecessor to Billings), the Shannon and Hall Company operated out of a tent in 1882. (Bottom) In Wichita, Kansas, Milo Kellogg, the first postmaster, also sold drugs and a variety of oils in addition to stamps. Dr. E. B. Allen was mayor and appointed Wyatt Earp city marshal.

Fred Fleishman's Drugstore in Tucson, Arizona Territory, advertised a line of trusses and shoulder braces, another facet of the cure-yourself philosophy of the period. Fleishman displayed show globes in his window and a mortar and pestle from his store front.

in the West had its special folk cures, many handed down from generation to generation and dispensed, most often, by elderly women in the community who had a penchant for that sort of thing.

Some of the "root and yarb" treatments contained the same drugs a doctor might use; but many of the pastes, poultices and potions were founded more on superstition than scientific fact. These do-it-yourself medicines were a thorn in the side of both druggists and physicians, but on the rough and rugged frontier, one had to expect almost anything—even a salve made of crushed bedbugs.

The medicines used by the pioneer practitioners de-

pended largely upon their training. The disciples of Samuel Hahnemann, the recognized founder of homeopathy, prescribed many drugs—but not much of any. The allopaths went in for heavy doses of calomel and ipecac. Botanic physicians were partial to herb and root concoctions. In general, though, most country doctors carried a small medicine case with a variety of remedies to treat the specific illnesses they knew something about. Their kits contained emetics (to induce vomiting), diaphoretics (for perspiration), cathartics (for purging), diuretics (to stimulate urination), sedatives, narcotics and tonics. It was also a rare saddlebag which didn't contain a liberal supply of whiskey, either

The G. Kellogg Drugstore in Seattle, Washington Territory, featured a wide selection of toiletries, including shaving mugs and brushes. The tidy establishment boasted gas lights and stools for customers when Theodore E. Peiser snapped this pre-1889 photo.

for the patient or the doctor himself.

As settlements stabilized and grew into cities, the professions of pharmacy and medicine tended to go their separate ways. Doctors and druggists alike had enough to do without doubling in brass; they became allies rather than competitors.

Actually, if drugstores had a turning point, it was probably in 1872 when George O. Guy (who was to become a prominent pharmacist in Seattle, Washington) accidentally invented the ice cream soda. According to the story, he worked part-time behind a fountain while he was attending the Philadelphia College of Pharmacy, and when he tried to fill an ice cream order for one customer and a soda water request for another, he inadvertently plopped the former into the latter. Before he could throw the mixture down the drain, one of the customers asked to taste it —and he liked it!

After that, drugstores were never quite the same.

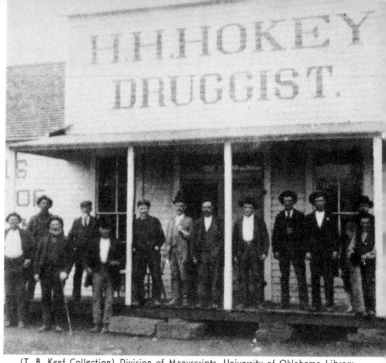

(Above) The H. H. Hokey Drugstore served the residents of Krebs, Indian Territory (Choctaw Nation), beginning in 1888. (Below) In Enid, Oklahoma Territory, the Evans Drugstore was cluttered and confined.

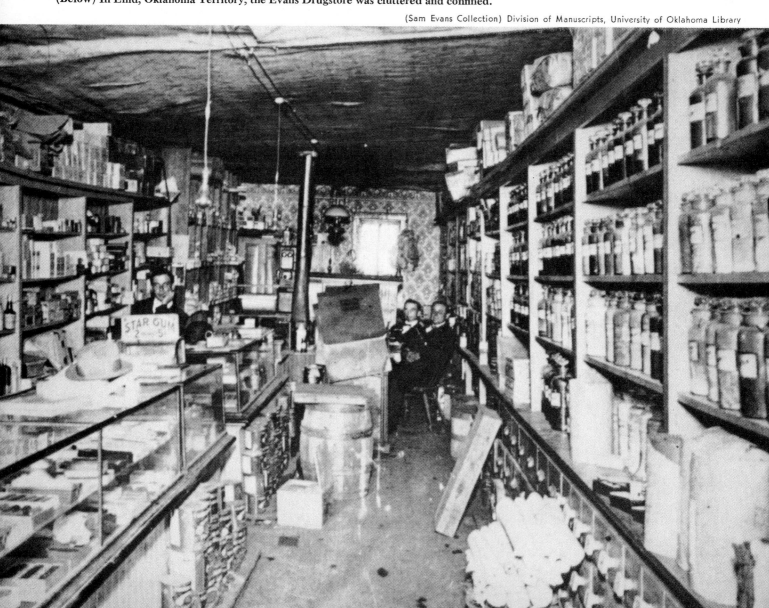

The Old Standbys

WHILE pioneer doctors had many drugs and medicines to choose from, the following were among the popular favorites:

Laudanum: Tincture of opium, for relief of pain and inflammation.

Ipecac: Preparation made from dried roots of a South American creeping plant, used as an emetic.

Jalap: Tuberous root of a Mexican plant, used as a cathartic or purge.

Tartar Emetic: Crystals of antimony and potassium tartrate, employed usually as a sedative or an emetic.

Dover's Powder: Powder consisting of opium, ipecac and sugar of milk, as a sedative or to cause sweating.

Calomel: Mercurous chloride, used as a laxative purge.

Blue Mass: Laxative made by rubbing up metallic mercury with licorice and other excipients.

Paregoric: Tincture of opium and camphor, to check diarrhea.

Nux Vomica: Beans of an East Indian tree which contain strychnine, used as a stimulant.

Belladonna: Leaves and root of the deadly nightshade containing atrophine, used as a stimulant and to decrease all secretions of the body except the urine.

Quinine: Alkaloid obtained from the bark of the Cinchona tree (Peruvian bark), used to treat malaria (ague) and as a tonic.

Morphine: The chief alkaloid of opium used primarily as a pain-killer.

Arnica: Dried flower heads of a plant native to the Old West, used as a tincture to relieve sprains and bruises.

Digitalis: Dried leaves of the Foxglove plant, used as a heart stimulant.

Seidlitz Powder: A pioneer effervescent anti-acid containing bitartrate of sodium and potassium, bicarbonate of sodium and tartaric acid.

Ergot: Derived from spawn of a fungus which grows in the flower of common rye, used to stimulate uterine contractions and in the treatment of certain hemorrhages.

Blaud's Pills: Carbonate of iron, given in cases of anemia.

Asafetida: A gum resin, used as a stimulant and carminative in the alimentary canal.

Picture credits (top to bottom): Nebraska State Historical Society; L. H. Jorud, Commercial Photo Shop, Helena, Montana; State Historical Society of Colorado; (S. D. Butcher Collection) Nebraska State Historical Society.

(Top to Bottom) D. W Tingley's drugstore in early-day Lincoln, Nebraska; in Helena, Montana, this customer might well have been ordering a bottle of Dr. Radway's Sarsaparillian Renovating Resolvent; Frank J. Lord operated the second oldest pharmacy in Denver; in Overton, Nebraska, the druggist was well prepared for the Christmas trade.

One of the earliest pharmacies in Denver was Graham's City Drugstore which looked like this shortly after the Civil War. Owner William Graham plastered his windows with posters promoting patent medicines, which, sad to say, were the most lucrative items on any druggist's shelves in those days.

(Above) Godbe, Pitts & Co., in Salt Lake City, was the first drugstore in Utah. In 1855 the owners offered their customers a variety of almanacs, through *The Deseret News*, "Free Gratis, for nothing at all." (Below) Brisley's was a well-stocked pharmacy in territorial Arizona.

KICKAPOO BY KICKAPOO INDIAN

(Opposite page) There was nothing like a good old-time medicine show to excite the natives—and sell barrels of patent medicine. This classic example of quackery in action was photographed in Marine, Minnesota, about the turn of the century. **(Above)** A traveling purveyor of Key Stone Balm peddled his magic ointment in Pasadena, California, in the late 1890s.

Quackery: By Truss and Tonic

". . . there is no cure for stupidity!"

HENRY E. SIGERIST, M.D.
The Johns Hopkins University

WHEN President Theodore Roosevelt signed the Federal Pure Food and Drug Act into law on June 30, 1906, he brought to a close a unique chapter in American medical history.

Pioneers in the Old West were particularly susceptible to the wiles of medicine show barkers and the fantastic advertisements which appeared in their tiny frontier newspapers.

"Diphtheria instantly relieved and permanently cured by using KURAKOFF, Nature's Life Preserver."

"Piso's Cure for Consumption has cured thousands."

"Aphroditine, the Celebrated French Cure, is sold on a positive guarantee to cure any form of nervous disease or any disorder of the generative organs of either sex."

There were absolutely no physical or mental ills for which the marvelous panaceas of the 1800s could not give "instant, lasting relief." Hysterics, wry neck, seminal weaknesses, bilious cholic, gravel, nervous derangement and green sickness were all curable with dollar-a-bottle tonics and restoratives.

There were many reasons why patent medicines caught on so well in the western country. One, of course, was man's continual quest for the cheap, quick, painless way to attain good health. Gullibility, ignorance and pure boredom were obvious factors. Then, there was the scarcity of qualified doctors, and in their absence, "granny" remedies and magic cure-alls were substituted. To make matters worse, many of the elixirs were concocted by greed-inspired men who could boast a medical degree; and some of the poorly trained physicians in country practice actually prescribed the pills and potions of the itinerant peddlers.

But an especially good reason was alcholic content!

Temperance workers who smashed whiskey bottles with utter abandon sipped medicinal bitters which were more booze than benefit. Rum-hating ministers and conscientious teetotalers were among the users of Hostetter's Celebrated Stomach Bitters (44.3% alcohol by volume), Peruna (28%), Parker's Tonic (41.6%), Lydia E. Pinkham's Vegetable Compound (20.6%) and Hoofland's "entirely vegetable" German Bitters (25.6%) It was a good business to be in—and many fortunes were made in the hey-day of quackery.

Dr. James Cook Ayer, with a medical degree from the University of Pennsylvania in 1841, bought a drugstore and began to manufacture a line of family remedies—which also included a hair invigorator. His name became a household word throughout the West as his factories produced "630,000 doses a day" of Ayer's Ex-

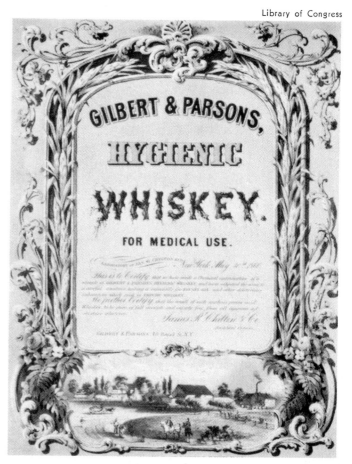

(Right) Whiskey was the all-purpose remedy on the frontier—antiseptic, anesthetic, pain-killer and courage-builder. Gilbert & Parsons made a point of emphasizing the medical values of their Hygienic brand. (Below) Patent medicine salesmen shouted their wares from the rooftops, literally and figuratively. This traveling barker drew a crowd of curious farmers in Ness County, Kansas.

tract of Sarsaparilla and other nostrums.

In the late 1800s no woman in America was more widely known than Lydia Estes Pinkham, school teacher, temperance worker and brewer of home remedies. Originally she gave away her elixir by the gallons, but when the panic of 1873 brought the Pinkhams to the brink of poverty, she began to accept payment for her "vegetable compound." In less than a decade her family was rolling in money.

Asa T. Soule—at various times a farmer, real estate promoter and shrewd salesman—bought a somewhat obscure formula, fortified it with alcohol and amassed a fortune with his famous Hop Bitters, "the invalid's friend and hope." No one, however, could match the imagination and showmanship of John E. (Doc) Healy and Charles H. (Texas Charlie) Bigelow. Their Kickapoo Indian Sagwa and other remedies attributed to native American tribesmen were known—and bought—from coast to coast, largely through the medium of the Kickapoo medicine show.

Dozens of other firms grew out of concoctions brewed on a kitchen range or in the back room of a

(Above) In Dodge City, Kansas, the carrying of firearms was strictly prohibited on the same signboard which advertised Prickly Ash Bitters. Patent medicines were sold in every nook and cranny of the Old West in an era of amazing gullibility. Medicine shows were lampooned, but the public went on buying just the same.

145

tiny drugstore. They were aided and abetted by a post-Civil War development in the newspaper business known as the "readyprint." Because frontier publishers were short of help, time and paper, imaginative suppliers began to provide sheets which were preprinted on one side with masses of patent medicine advertising. From Chicago the A. N. Kellogg syndicate alone carried these cure-all messages to some 1,400 small country newspapers through their so-called "patent insides."

The medicine shows, of course, had a natural appeal to the entertainment-starved pioneers in scattered prairie villages and mountain hamlets. They gawked at the Indian chiefs and dancing girls, volunteered to have aching teeth pulled free, fell for the shill who was always there to buy the first bottle—and they forked over their hard-earned dollars for every imaginable kind of salve, syrup and solution.

No wonder the legitimate doctors and their embryonic medical associations were outraged. Things were bad enough without competition from do-it-yourself medication. From an economic standpoint, sodbusters and squatters found it cheaper to look for

health in a bottle than to summon a doctor who might be a two- or three-day ride away. Ultimately—when the physician *had* to be called—it was often too late for him to do any good. Not infrequently he got the blame for a death which directly or indirectly should have been laid to a patent panacea.

Not that all proprietary drugs were harmful! Many were simply *harmless;* they didn't hurt nor help. Their biggest damage came through delay of proper treatment. Some, however, were down-right poisonous, being concocted by transient charlatans from whatever ingredients they could get their hands on. Alcoholic and opium addictions were not unusual results from the so-called "bracers" and pain-killers. These, in turn, brought about still another market: cures for the addicted. Colden's Liquid Beef Tonic, which was sold "for the treatment of alcoholic habit," itself contained 26.5% alcohol. Keeley Institutes, with their "double

There were literally hundreds of elixirs for an ailing individual to choose from in the hey-day of the do-it-yourself medicine. Many of the so-called bitters were so potent that after the Pure Food and Drug Law was inaugurated in 1906, they had to be sold as alcoholic beverages.

Wyoming State Archives and Historical Department

National Library of Medicine

Alcoholism and addictions to drugs were serious problems of the 19th century. The availability of opium without prescription and its excessive use by some of the poorly trained practitioners were largely responsible for the latter. "Taking the cure" became a household expression as special institutes were founded to help sufferers break the habit. Dr. Leslie E. Keeley promoted his "double chloride of gold" treatment throughout the West, while Dr. S. B. Collins of LaPorte, Indiana, offered Theriaki, "the painless cure for the opium and liquor habits."

chloride of gold" remedies, appeared in the larger cities throughout the West.

With the patent medicines came other phases of quackery. The variety was limited only by the imagination of the inventors and the gullibility of the suffering. "Doctors of gadgetry" preyed especially upon those who were clutching at medical straws to cure hopeless cases. Magnetic rings, electric belts, inhalators, vaporizors, trusses and wierd machinery which would have done Rube Goldberg proud flooded the market. Medicinal hankies, restorative amulets and even a ridiculous device called The Health Jolting Chair found ready purchasers.

Not to be confused with legitimate hospitals, sanitaria and clinics were the health institutes, laboratories and dispensaries which advertised quick cures for almost everything. Special targets, though, were the secret deficiencies of manhood. Dr. R. F. Price in his Denver clinic offered to treat "all diseases arising from the indiscretions of early youth" and guaranteed to forfeit $1,000 for any case of seminal weakness he accepted and failed to cure.

There were so-called doctors who guaranteed to cure cancer and other internal ailments "without the knife." Cancer pastes were prominent. "Mad stones" to cure hydrophobia were available for a price. Slickers were everywhere, and in the Barnum tradition, there were always suckers to be had.

In Oklahoma and Kansas before the turn of the century two fast-talking con-men swindled hundreds of unsuspecting citizens (mostly women) with an imaginative patent medicine scheme. One of the "doctors" would appear in a town and spend a week or so visiting all the chronic cases, hypochondriacs and any

147

The patent medicine makers reached almost everywhere in the vegetable kingdom to create unique formulas for their nostrums. Celery compounds were big sellers, and even the lowly dandelion found a commercial use in Leis' special tonic advertised by this Georgetown, Colorado, drugstore in the 1880s.

other potential push-overs he could find. He was glib and sympathetic, and as he chatted with them he wrote down all their symptoms, how long they had been suffering and, of course, his analysis of their ability to pay. People were pleased because he listened, and he didn't try to force his medicines on them. Then, with his research completed, he'd leave town.

Not long afterwards, his henchman would appear, and this second "doctor" would set up an office and advertise extensively in the community newspaper. Soon the same complainers came to see him. A nurse (also part of the team) would get the patient's name, and the "doctor" would proceed to look up the individual's history secured the week before by his cohort.

When the victim was ushered in, the smooth-talking quack would rattle off the patient's symptoms in a wise, professional manner. The dupe, of course, would be amazed at the "doctor's" brilliance, and when a guaranteed cure was offered—payable in advance, of course—the response was immediate. By the time the phoney physician had gone through his entire list, he would have a bundle of money, all for a few bottles of cheap tonic which he gave to each caller as the first step in his treatment. And that would also be the last, too, because the "doctor" would suddenly disappear— off to the next frontier town where his partner had prepared a new clientele.

Not to be overlooked were the faith-practitioners,

Denver Public Library Western Collection

Palo Alto (Calif.) Public Library

Medical gimmicks provided quacks with other hot sales items. Trusses, health hankies and cure-all necklaces were snapped up by eager buyers. Doctor Horne's "best electric belt on earth" was guaranteed to cure everything from torpid liver to lost vigor. Elixirs, like Scott's Emulsion so poetically advertised above, were equally all-promising. (Below) Wei De Meyer's Catarrh Cure was offered from the gas lights of this Georgetown, Colorado, pharmacy.

Denver Public Library Western Collection

strange mystics like Bill the Healer, who operated in Wyoming during the 1870s. When Bill appeared in a strange saloon, invariably someone (his shill) would fall desperately ill. Promptly the Healer would apply his magic touch, and the victim would be restored. After that, the opportunities for other cures (which included relieving the patient of his money) soon presented themselves.

Almost everybody got into the quick-cure act. The populace was ripe for the plucking. After all, who wanted to be sick when a bottle of Samaritan Nervine would (to quote the label) cure:

Epileptic fits, spasms, convulsions, St. Vitus Dance, vertigo, hysterics, insanity, apoplexy, paralysis, rheumatism, neuralgia and all nervous diseases; female weakness, general debility, eucorrhea or whites, painful menstruation, ulceration of the uterus, internal heat, gravel, inflammation and irritability of the bladder; alcoholism, drunkenness and the habit of opium eating;

149

nervous dyspepsia, palpitation of the heart, asthma, bronchitis, scrofula, syphilis, diseases of the kidneys and the urinary organs; nervous debility caused by the indiscretions of youth.

No wonder author Stewart Holbrook called it "the Golden Age of Quackery," and no wonder the serious-minded doctors were continually upset by the charlatanism around them. In the end, the quacks and the patent medicine peddlers over-stepped their bounds, and with the turn of the new century, the hue and cry against them rose from all directions. The Pure Food and Drug Act of 1906 was one of the major results.

While the new law did not automatically eliminate the evils of quackery, it at least served notice on the medical con-men that their days of unlimited freedom were over. As the ensuing years were to prove, quick-money operators exist in every generation, laws or no laws. But in the wild-and-woolly West of the 19th century, there were no restrictions whatsoever—and the heartless quacks took full advantage of the situation!

The Bitters and the Sweets

THE variety of patent medicines available to pioneers on the western frontier was seemingly unending. Drugstore shelves literally bulged with unusual bottles with fancy labels and fancier titles. The remedies ran the gamut from worthlessness to dangerously harmful. One—when the truth was finally known—consisted of nothing more than sugar water. Others, because of their cathartic action, brought some relief—if they weren't taken for the wrong reason.

The following litany of 19th century nostrums is by no means complete. It does, however, indicate the extent to which do-it-yourself medicine had blanketed the known ills of the day. Some of the products are still available—but the manufacturers have since fulfilled the requirements of the Pure Food and Drug Law and, in most cases, have upgraded their formulae.

Dr. Acker's English Elixir
Dr. A. W. Allen's Southern Liniment
Anderson's Pills
Aphroditine
August Flower Bitters
Autumn Leaf Extract for Females
Ayer's Ague Cure
Ayer's Cathartic Pills
Ayer's Cherry Pectoral
Ayer's Extract of Sarsaparilla
Baker's Panacea
Barkers' Nerve & Bone Liniment
Barker's Powder
Barney's Cocoa Castorine
Dr. Bateman's Pectoral Drops
O. Battista's Antilepsis
Black-Draught
Bogle's Hyperion Fluid
Boker's Stomach Bitters
Boschee's German Syrup
C. C. Bristol's Sarsaparilla
Brown's Arnica Salve
Brown's Bronchial Troches
Brown's Cough Balsam
Dr. Brown's Male Fern Vermifuge
Brown's Pepsin Tonic
Dr. Brown's Renovating Pills
Dr. Brown's Woodland Balm
Dr. John Bull's Compound Cedron Bitters
Dr. John Bull's Compound of Wild Cherry
Dr. John Bull's Cough Syrup
Dr. John Bull's Sarsaparilla
California Waters of Life
Carbolate of Tar
Carter's Spanish Mixture
Celerena
Celery-Cola
Celery Malt Compound (Sears, Roebuck)
Celery-Vesce
Centaur Liniment
Chamber's Remedy For Intemperance

Sir James Clarke's Celebrated Female Pills
Colden's Liquid Beef Tonic
Columbian Syrup
Cooper's Magic Balm
Cram's Fluid Lightning
Crossman's Specific
Darby's Prophylactic Fluid
Dr. Davis' Painless Catarrh Specific
Perry Davis' Vegetable Pain Killer
Dead Shot Vermifuge
Dr. Juan Delamarre's Specific Pills
Dimmitt's Cough Balsam
Doyle's Bitters
Drake's Plantation Bitters
Duffey's Pure Malt Whiskey
Dr. Easterly Sarsaparilla
Electro-Tonic
Dr. J. C. Fahey's Pepsin Anodyne
Dr. Fahnestock's Celebrated Vermifuge
    and Liquid Opeldoc
Father John's Medicine
Fosgate's Anodyne Cordial
Frese's Hamburg Tea
Gilbert & Parsons Hygienic Whiskey
Godfrey's Cordial
Dr. Goulard's Celebrated Infallible Fit
    Powders
Graefenberg's Catholicon
Gray's Ointment
Green Mountain Ointment
Greene's Nervura
Dr. William Hall's Balsam
Hall's Catarrh Cure
Harlem Oil
Healey's Liver Pad
Henry's Magnesia
Dr. Herrick's Sugar-Coated Pills
Hinkley's Bone Liniment
Holloway's Worm Confections
The Home Stomach Bitters
Honey Pectoral

Hood's Sarsaparilla
Hoofland's German Bitters
Hooker's Wigwam Tonic
Soule's Hop Bitters
Soule's Hop Cure
Hostetter's Celebrated Stomach Bitters
Howe's Arabian Tonic
Howland's Balsamic Cordial
Hungarian Balsam
Hyatt's Life Balsam
Indian Cough Cure
Indian Cough Syrup
Jackson's Embrocation
Jacob's Cordial
Dr. Jaynes' Carminative
Dr. Jaynes' Expectorant
Dr. Jaynes' Sanative Pills
Dr. Joinville's Specific Pills
Ka-Ton-Ka
Ka-Tar-No (Peruna)
Old Dr. Kaufman's Great Sulfur Bitters
Key Stone Balm
Kickapoo Indian Cough Cure
Kickapoo Indian Oil
Kickapoo Indian Prairie Plant
Kickapoo Indian Sagwa
Kickapoo Indian Salve
Kickapoo Indian Worm Killer
Kidder's Cordial
Kidney-Wort
Dr. Kilmer's Swamp Root
Dr. King's New Discovery for Consumption
King's Prepared Prescription
Kookman's Bitters
Kurakoff
Dr. Leeson's Tiger Oil
Lithia Waters
Luciana Cordial
Lyon's Kathairon
Donald McKay's Indian Worm Eradicator

McLane's Vermifuge
Medicated Oil Silk Bandage
Mensman's Peptonized Beef Tonic
Mexican Mustang Liniment
Dr. Miles' New Heart Cure
Dr. Mintie's Vital Restorative
Modoc Oil
Moffat's Bitters
Dr. Morse's Indian Root Pills
Moxie Nerve Food
Munyon's Blood Cure
Murray's Fluid Magnesia
Murray's Specific
Nez Perce Catarrh Snuff
Ocean Weed Heart Remedy
Old Sachem Bitters
Orchis Extract
Organo
Osgood's Chologue
Oxien Health Tablets
Oxien Laxative Pills
Oxien Nazone Salve
Oxien Pile Treatment
Pagliano Syrup
Paine's Celery Compound
Paregoric Elixir
Pareira's Remedy
Park Obesity Pills
Parker's Tonic
Parks' Tea
Pasteur's Concentrate of Herbs
Peruna
Peruvian Bitters
Phyto-Gingerin
Dr. Pierce's Favorite Prescription
Dr. Pierce's Golden Medical Discovery
Pine Pinon Cough Cure
Pink Pills For Pale People

Piso's Cure for Consumption
Pitcher's Castoria
Lady Poor's Ointment
Potter's Catholicon
Prickly Ash Bitters
Prompt Parilla Liver Pills
Dr. Radway's Sarsaparillian Renovating
    Resolvent
Dr. Raphael's Cordial Invigorant
Dr. Raphael's Galvanic Love Powders
Rich's Tasteless Chill Tonic and King of
    Malaria
Richardson's Concentrated Sherry Wine
    Bitters
Ripans Tabules
Roback's Blood and Liver Pills
Roger's Liverwort Tar
Dr. Sage's Catarrh Remedy
St. Jacob's Oil
Samaritan Nervine
Sanford's Invigorator
Sapanule
Scott's Emulsion
Scovill's Blood & Liver Syrup
Dr. D. H. Seelye's Liquid Catarrh
    Remedy
Shaker Extract of Roots
Shiloh's Consumption Cure
Dr. Simm's Arsenic Complexion Wafers
Dr. Simms' Safe Periodical Wafers
Simmons Liver Regulator
Smith's Asthma Cure
Dr. Steers' Chemical Opodeldoc
Dr. Stephany's Gold Tincture
Stoughton's London Bitters
Swayne's Ointment
Syrup of Figs
Syrup of Salza of De Angelis

Thayer's Compound Extract of Sarsapa-
    rilla
Thayer's Slippery Elm Lozenges
Theriaki
Dr. Thomson's Celebrated Eye Water
Tiger Fat
Ton-Ko-Ko Tonic
Dr. Townsend's Cholera Balm
Dr. Townsend's King of Coughs
Dr. Townsend's Remedy For Catarrh
Dr. Townsend's Sarsaparilla
Dr. Townsend's Wizard Oil
Turlington's Balsam of Life
Tuscarora Rice
Tutt's Pills for Tired Liver
Vegetine
Vermilyea's Oil of Life
Vinol, Wine of Cod-Liver Oil
Vital Sparks
Dr. Walker's California Vinegar Bitters
Ward's Anodyne Pearls
Warm Spring Consumption Cure
Warner's Safe Kidney and Liver Cure
War Paint Ointment
Webber's Magic Compound
Wei De Meyers Catarrh Cure
Whiskol
Whitcomb's Remedy
Faith Whitcomb's Nerve Bitters
White Star Secret Liquor Cure
    (Sears, Roebuck)
J. P. Whitwell's Chemical Embrocation
Wilson's Panacea
Dr. Wilson's Restorative Remedies
Wine of Cardui
Mrs. Winslow's Soothing Syrup
Worlds Catarrh Cure

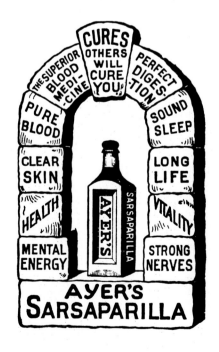

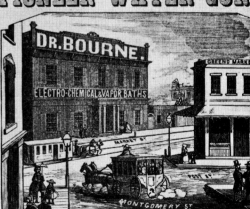

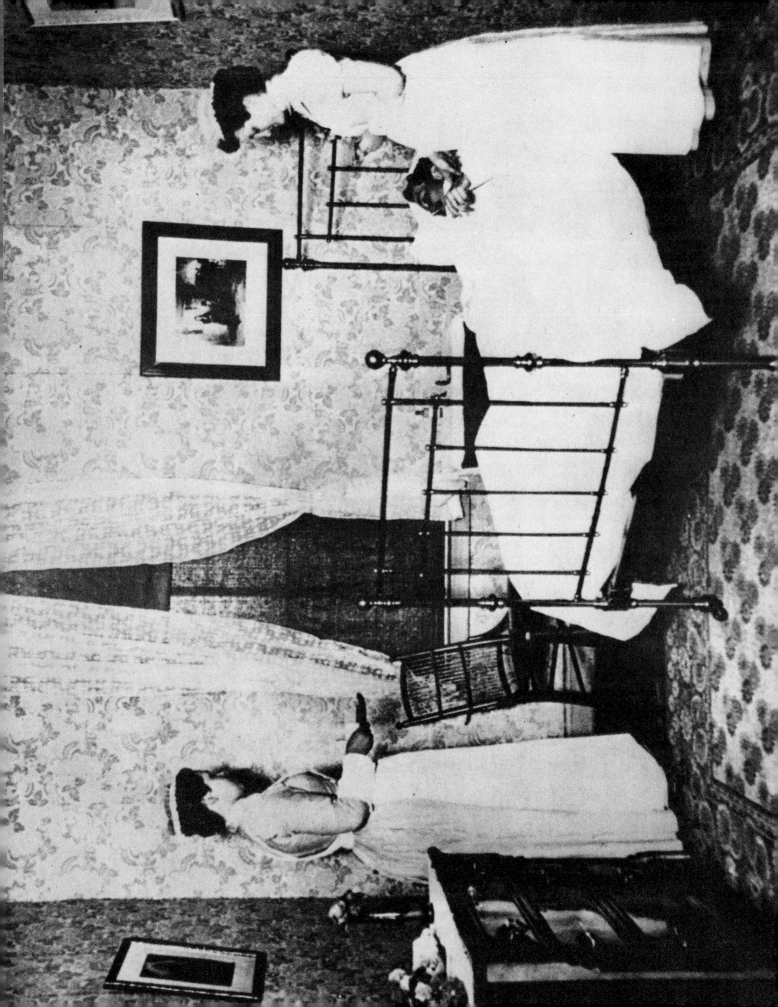

(Opposite page) Minnesota Historical Society   (Above) State Historical Society of Colorado

(Opposite page) In earlier days, nurses were simply menial servants, with no education and little appreciation of sanitation or medical care. By the end of the 19th century they had achieved both training and status as allies of the physicians they served. This picture was taken at St. Luke's Hospital in Duluth, Minnesota. (Above) Though not an Old West practitioner, Dr. Florence R. Sabin of Colorado exemplified the role of women in pioneer medicine. As a graduate of Johns Hopkins University in 1900, she gained world-wide fame as a teacher, physician and research worker.

Never Call Them the Weaker Sex

It matters little whether men or women have the more brains. All we need to do to exert our proper influence is to use all the brains we have.

Florence Rena Sabin, M.D.

No story of medicine in the Old West would be complete without including the contributions made by the courageous ladies who served in the far reaches of American civilization as doctors, nurses, mid-wives and "grannies." They delivered babies, battled epi-demics, built hospitals (literally and figuratively), and they brought a feminine dimension to a profession which no doubt would have been somewhat less com-passionate and more clinical without them.

For a woman to become a doctor before the Civil War was an accomplishment of uncommon zeal. The preceptor system was virtually barred to young girls, no matter how dedicated or talented they might have been. The earliest medical schools made determined efforts to maintain an all-male enrollment. Still, in

155

When Elizabeth Blackwell won her degree from the Geneva (N.Y.) Medical College in 1849, she proved that women were fully capable of a role they had long been denied. Though she broke medical precedents, "lady doctors" were not generally accepted until well after the Civil War. Among the courageous women who practiced in the Old West were Dr. Romania B. Pratt (left above), first of her sex in Utah, and Dr. Martha Hughes Cannon (right above), who established Utah's first training school for nurses and in 1896 became a state senator. (Below) In 1882 the women of the Mormon Relief Society—including two physicians—established Deseret Hospital in the adobe building where the Sisters of the Holy Cross had formerly cared for the sick.

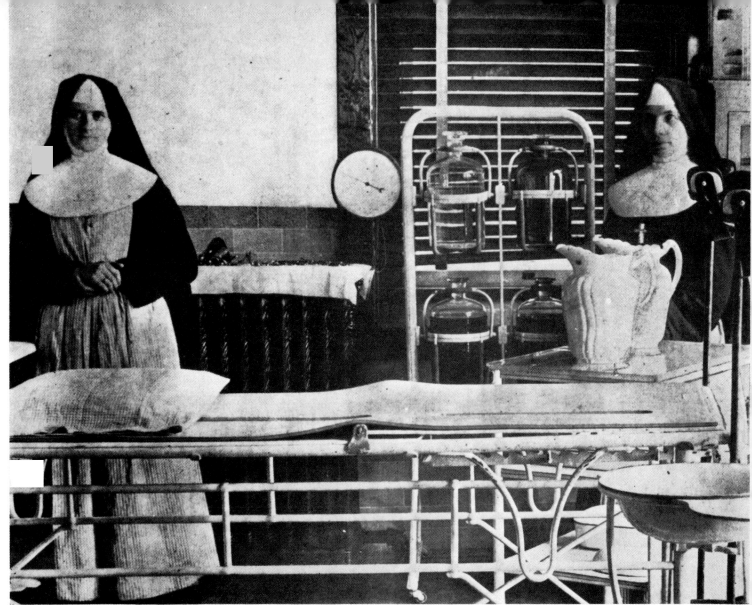

Sisters Joseph and Constantine were justifiably proud of the operating room of St. Mary's Hospital in 1893. Dr. Charles Mayo was particularly instrumental in the selection and purchase of the new equipment which was brought to Rochester, Minnesota, from Berlin. Throughout the Old West, Catholic nuns played a leading role in the development of hospitals.

1849, Elizabeth Blackwell was graduated from Geneva (N.Y.) Medical College, the first woman to receive a doctor of medicine degree from a school in the United States. The following year Lydia Folger Fowler earned her M.D. at the Rochester (N.Y.) Eclectic Medical College. That same year—1850—the Women's Medical College of Pennsylvania opened its doors, the first such school in America.

At Harvard, though, when Harriet K. Hunt—who had been practicing medicine for 15 years without a diploma—tried to gain admission to the medical school in 1850, she was thwarted by student objections. Dean Oliver Wendell Holmes and the faculty at first approved her acceptance, but then the male class members submitted two protesting resolutions which read:

"*Resolved,* That no woman of true delicacy would be willing in the presence of men to listen to the dis-

cussions of the subjects that necessarily come under consideration of the student of medicine.

"*Resolved,* That we object to having the company of any female forced upon us, who is disposed to unsex herself, and to sacrifice her modesty by appearing with men in the medical lecture room."

Rather than face a revolt of the young men of Harvard, the faculty changed its mind and Doctor Hunt, still diploma-less, was turned away.

While men ranted about the woman's place being in the home, a new era had dawned in medicine, and the effects were soon to felt on the western frontier. At first, though, a diploma was of little consequence to the wives and mothers accompanying the wagon trains beyond the Mississippi. Without formal training, they nursed the sick "by instinct and intuition" Typical was 17-year-old Elizabeth Perry, who left Iowa for Oregon

157

in 1845. With no doctor in the group, the teen-ager assumed the role, serving as mid-wife, collecting herbs and roots for medicinal brews and generally ministering to the health needs of the caravan. Later she put up a sign, "Mrs. E. Perry, Doctress," and for more than half a century she practiced mid-wifery and her own unschooled brand of medicine in the St. Helens region of Oregon.

As early as 1855, Dr. Martha Spalding Thurston, graduate of the Boston Female Medical College, arrived in San Francisco via the Isthmus to open an office with her physician-husband. There were a few others, too—with and without diplomas—who ventured into the western territories during the pre-Civil War period. Among them were five nuns—Sisters of Charity of Providence—who traveled from Montreal to the Isthmus of Panama, crossed it on foot and then sailed

Frank Leslie's Illustrated Newspaper, April 16, 1870

In spite of male outrage and general public disapproval, women began to invade the medical ranks after the Civil War. Because many established colleges would not admit women, several all-female schools were opened. This sketch depicts the anatomical lecture room of the New York Medical College for Women.

(Left) Among the women physicians who practiced successfully in the early West was Dr. Lillian Heath of Rawlins, Wyoming. In 1888 while studying with a preceptor, she wore mannish type clothing "to avoid talk." She also carried two pistols. Later she received a degree from the College of Physicians and Surgeons in Keokuk, Iowa. (Below) Dr. Georgia Arbuckle Fix and her medicine kit were well known to many pioneer families in western Nebraska.

Nebraska State Historical Society

Neal E. Miller Collection

158

(Below) Wives of pioneer physicians deserve their own little niche in the history of frontier medicine. Many of them—like Mrs. W. W. Mayo—assisted their husbands directly as nurses and aides. (Above) Though she didn't qualify by training or general reputation, Calamity Jane has been mentioned several times in memoirs and early-day newspapers as serving in a nursing capacity. The picture shown here was taken in Gilt Edge, Montana, in the mid-1880s.

northward to Fort Vancouver on the Columbia River which they reached on December 8, 1856. They were not doctors but medical pioneers who ultimately were to bring hospital care to numerous communities throughout the Pacific Northwest. Two years earlier six Irish Sisters of Mercy were nursing cholera victims in San Francisco. In virtual anonymity, other small groups of nuns appeared elsewhere in the West to establish hospitals and to provide care for the sick and suffering.

Everywhere, though, the women of medicine found themselves the target of male jealousy and scorn; the sisters bore the additional burden of religious intolerance. But the causes of women's suffrage were advancing, and the doctors and nurses in petticoats were in the forefront of the movement, either directly or indirectly. A major milestone had its beginning on October 21, 1854, when Florence Nightingale sailed from England for the Crimean Peninsula with 38 nurses. Her mission was to reorganize the British military hospitals which had been publicly deplored because of their gross inefficiency and filth. Her unusual achievements

Midwives were a virtual institution on the western frontier. Like country doctors, their "practices" ranged far and wide. Few had any particular training; they got by on experience, common sense and feminine intuition. Josephine Catherine Chatterly Wood was known as "Aunt Jody" to hundreds of pioneer Utahans whose children she helped bring into the world. All saddled up, she was probably ready to ride to another confinement.

—in the face of monstrous obstacles—made her a national heroine and focused a world spotlight on the role of women in the care of the wounded and the sick. In 1860 she established her famed school of nursing at St. Thomas' Hospital in London.

The story of Florence Nightingale reverberated around the globe and further inspired the suffrage activities in America. During the Civil War some 2,000 female nurses—including nuns—served valiantly; a special congressional act in 1859 had granted them a munificent salary of fifty cents a day. After Appomattox, this nucleus of experienced women did much to stimulate interest in nursing, and yet, it was 1873 before the Bellevue Hospital in New York started a training school according to the Nightingale principles.

Meanwhile, in that same year the Toland Medical College of San Francisco became the Medical Depart-

ment of the University of California and in 1876 conferred a degree upon Lucy M. Field Wanzer, a 33-year-old school teacher who became the first woman to be graduated in medicine on the Pacific Coast. The next year two sisters—Angela L. and Ella A. J. Ford—received degrees from the Willamette University Medical Department in Salem, Oregon.

In spite of continuing prejudice, more and more women pursued medical educations. By 1870, when the University of Michigan became the first state institution to make its medical school coeducational, some 600 lady doctors were practicing in the United States. Many were so-called "irregulars"—homeopaths, hydropaths and eclectics—simply because admission to regular schools had been denied them. At first they tended to specialize in the treatment of women and children. Of this, male physicians were less resentful. Later, though, many of them were called upon to fill every imaginable role in their profession. Dr. Mary Babcock Moore, for instance, was physician for the Gold Leaf Mining Company in Montana. In her practice, she rode horseback over narrow mountain trails to reach and treat her patients. Like her male counterparts, Dr. Jennie Murphy of Yankton, South Dakota, used team and buggy to make her country calls, often waking to find herself in the barn after her horses had brought her safely home while she dozed through a long night-time ride.

If female doctors had a difficult time winning acceptance, nurses (even with the help of Florence Nightingale) had it tougher still. Through most of the 19th century their duties were considered menial rather than professional. They cleaned chimneys, carried in the winter coal, mopped floors and cooked meals. They were, according to one newspaper report, "sworn at by surgeons . . . abused by patients, insulted if old and ill-favored, talked flippantly to if middle-aged

(Right) Mother Joseph of the Sisters of Charity of Providence was an amazing woman. In the Pacific Northwest she designed and built many hospitals and schools. She even laid bricks with her own hands, and then went on begging missions to insure that the hospitals would not fail for lack of money. (Below) Another pioneer midwife was Hilda Anderson Erickson, on the white horse, who practiced in Tooele County, Utah.

(Below) Utah State Historical Society

(Above) Washington State Hospital Association

and good-humoured, and tempted and seduced if young and well-looking." A training school rule book of that period said that "any nurse who smoked or had her hair done at a beauty parlor gave adequate reason to suspect her intentions." On the other hand, not all nurses were the poetically-pictured "angels of mercy." Until professional schools were established (there were only 15 of them in the United States in 1880 with less than 350 students), the lowliness of the station attracted many untrained and uncultured females. Patient-beating was not uncommon, and promiscuity was a continuing problem.

Oddly enough, the very women who contributed so much to pioneer medicine—the religious sisters—had a somewhat negative effect on the advancement of nursing in the early years. Bound by vows of poverty, the

(Below) Nurses were prim and pert at St. Luke's Hospital, St. Paul, Minnesota, in the late 1880s. (Right) At the Northwestern Hospital for Women and Children in Minneapolis, a "ministering angel" brought comfort and security to those who needed it most.

(All pictures this page) Minnesota Historical Society

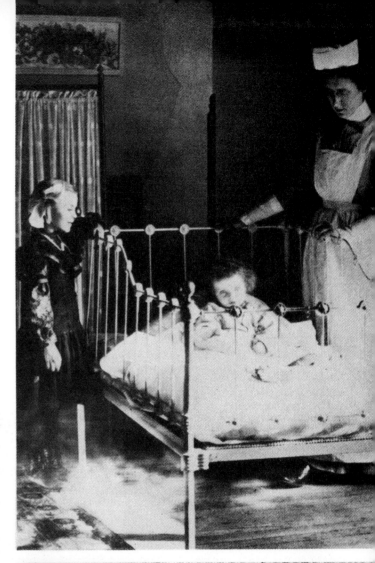

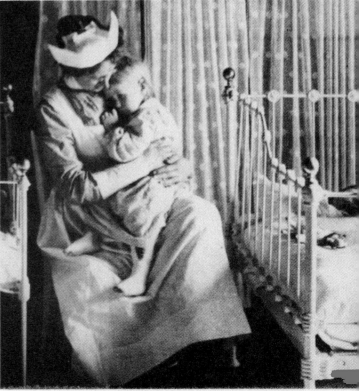

162

nuns gave totally of themselves in charity and mercy. Without pay, they labored endlessly, not only caring for the sick but performing all the lowly tasks asked of them. They begged in the streets on behalf of their struggling hospitals. They worked for pennies in private homes to raise funds for medicine and blankets. Needless to say, their contributions to humanity were outstanding—but not many lay women were capable of matching them in humility and self-denial.

These disparities, however, worked themselves out in time, and by the latter years of the century, the nuns were responsible for some of the finest training schools in the West, graduating hundreds of professional nurses to collaborate with country doctors from Omaha to the Olympic Peninsula.

In the meantime, women were rising to the occasion wherever nursing or doctoring services were needed. With the knowledge she had gained from her physician-father, Mrs. L. C. Smith of Carbon, Wyoming, assumed the role of doctor and—according to the archives of the Union Pacific Coal Company—"dosed

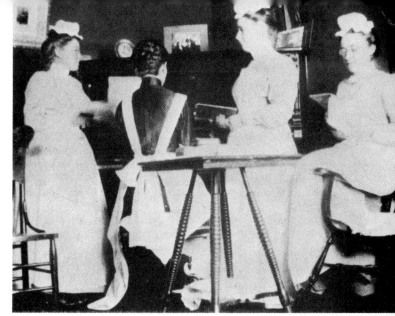

(Above) Nurses at Columbus Hospital in Great Falls, Montana, relaxed around a piano during off-duty hours. (Below) There were even a few lady pharmacists like this young lady in Denver at the turn of the century.

and sympathized her patients into recovery." The *Deadwood (S.D.) Pioneer* of July 13, 1876, carried this interesting item about one of the Old West's most flamboyant and controversial characters:

> The man Warren, who was stabbed on lower Main Street Wednesday night, is doing quite well under the care of Calamity Jane, who has kindly undertaken the job of nursing him. There's lots of humanity in Calamity, and she is deserving of much praise for the part she has taken in this particular case.

Two years later Calamity reputedly added to her nursing laurels by visiting the homes of smallpox victims during an epidemic in Deadwood when no one else would go near them. Florence Nightingale's statement that "at one time or another every woman is a nurse" was literally all-inclusive.

If there were unsung heroines of frontier medicine, the wives of the doctors were probably most deserving of the honor. They were called upon to make unusual sacrifices in behalf of their husbands' profession. All were not able to stand the gaff, but those who were shared in the satisfaction of a noble calling—if not substantial monetary rewards. Louise Abigail Mayo not

(Worden Collection) Wells Fargo History Room, San Francisco

only raised two of the nation's most prominent physicians, but she learned medicine, too, by working shoulder-to-shoulder with her spouse and by reading

(Above) San Francisco's German Hospital was founded before the Civil War by the German Benevolent Society. The name was later changed to Franklin Hospital when the animosities of the World War cast suspicion on all things Teutonic. (Below) Two well-starched nurses posed with a horse-drawn ambulance in early-day Portland, Oregon.

Shepard Ambulance Service, Seattle, Washington

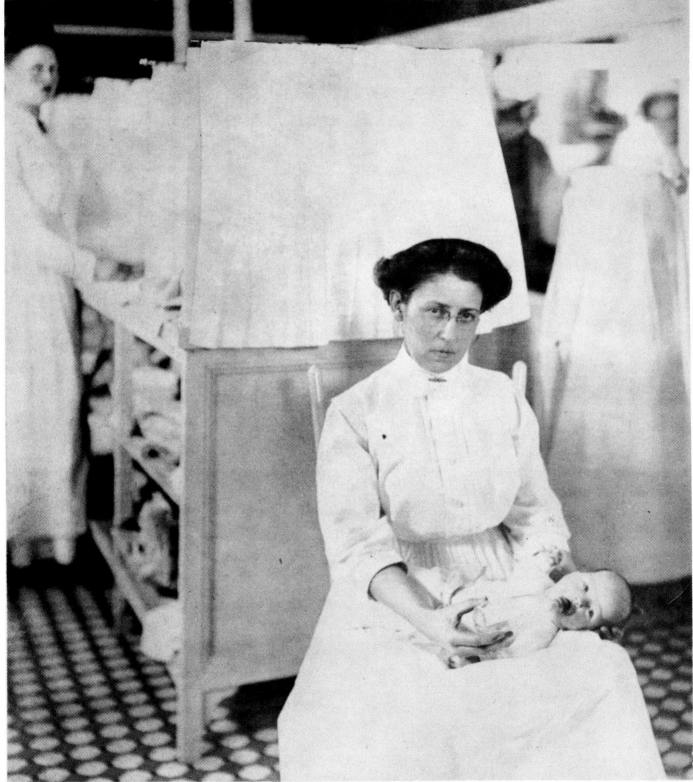

In 1900 this white-clad young lady was almost symbolic of her profession. Florence Nightingale had achieved a totally new respect for nursing almost a half-century before, but it took many years to break down old prejudices and habits, to establish worthwhile training schools and finally to provide physicians with co-workers they could depend upon for stability and skill.

his books and journals. She reduced fractures, applied splints and prescribed simple remedies "to tide folks over" when her husband was away. Her famous son, Dr. Charles Mayo, couldn't have paid her a greater compliment when he said: "Mother was a real good doctor herself."

Many other wives did as much and more. They were all involved in the same unending battle against sickness and death. They were allies of the pioneer nurses, the dedicated nuns, the early women doctors, the midwives and even the grandmothers who hopefully dispensed the unusual concoctions of their forefathers. In the 19th century the women of medicine never did win the complete approbation of their male contemporaries; they did, however, prepare the way for the generations to come. No longer would young ladies have to stand hopelessly in line in front of a medical school which wouldn't accept them, nor would they have to wear mannish clothing or carry pistols for protection as they tried to practice the profession of their choice.

One thing they proved conclusively: In medicine there is no such thing as the weaker sex! In 1875 Dr. A. E. Regensburger of San Francisco, in typical male tone, addressed the California State Medical Society regarding the women physicians it was preparing to admit to membership. "Taken as a whole," he said, "they probably never will amount to much."

Doctor Regensburger may have been one of the Bear State's first and foremost skin specialists, but about women he knew very little!

(Above) After two years the graduates of the Wichita (Kans.) Training School for Nurses got a diploma, $100 and a lifetime career. (Below) Nurses of Sacred Heart Hospital in Yankton, South Dakota, marched in a community parade.

"Not Wrinkled Hags Are We..."

Our art is learned by dames of gentle blood,
   Who sit with patient toil and lips contract,
If so they may relieve one human pang.
   The ghastly wound appals us not, nor yet
The raging fury of the moonstruck brain.
   Not wrinkled hags are we, with corded veins
Croaking with spells the midnight watches through
   But some are fair as She, the vestal mother.

ELIZABETH OAKES SMITH, 1850

167

Generally, the pioneer women physicians specialized in the treatment of women and children. The crusty miners, ranchers and railroad men of the frontier were not about to consult a "lady doctor." But the women of medicine persisted to the ultimate advantage of everyone. Some physicians in petticoats, like Dr. Ellis Reynolds Shipp of Utah, were responsible for the vastly improved training of nurses.

168

"Granny Remedies"

"GRANNY MEDICINE" was not quackery, as such. It was a strange conglomeration of superstition, religious fervor and simple ignorance—but it was practiced with great faith and not for financial gain.

Some of the treatments actually brought relief, espe-cially the herb teas and drawing poultices, but mostly they were little better than a rabbit's foot or a four-leaf clover. Their greatest evil was delay of proper medical attention. Here are a few typical examples of frontier do-it-yourself remedies.

Oil of geese, wolves, bears or polecats for rheumatism.
Poultice of slippery elm and Indian meal for burns.
Ointment of crushed sheep sorrel leaves and gunpowder for skin cancer.
Mashed cabbage for ulcer or cancer in breasts.
Mashed snails and earthworms in water for diphtheria.
Salve of lard and brimstone for itch.
Common salt with scrapings from pewter spoons for worms.
Boiled pumpkin seed tea for stomach worms.
Scorpion oil as a diuretic in venereal disease.
Tea made from steeping dried chicken gizzard linings in hot water for stomach ache.
Tonic made by soaking half a bucket of rusty nails in vinegar as a blood puri-fier.
Wood ashes or cobwebs to staunch bleeding.
Brandy and red pepper for cholera.
Mashed potato poultice to draw out the core of a boil.
Mold scraped from cheese or old bread for open sores.
A bag of asafetida worn around the neck to cure a cold.
Fried heart of rattlesnake or skunk meat to cure consumption.
To remove warts, rub them with green walnuts, bacon rind or chicken feet.
Carry an onion in your pocket to prevent smallpox.

169

Poultice of flaxseed for pneumonia.

Carry a horse chestnut to ward off rheumatism.

Owl broth to cure whooping cough.

Scratch gum with iron nail till it bleeds, then drive nail into wooden beam to relieve toothache.

Boiled toads to treat heart disease and dropsy.

Burnt sponge to treat goiter.

Soap and sugar poultice for boils.

Gold filings in honey to restore energy.

For pyorrhea, rinse the mouth with a liniment of gum myrrh, golden seal and red pepper.

Watermelon seeds boiled in water to treat kidney trouble.

Blood of a "bessie bug" dropped in the ear to cure earache.

Wrap legs in brown paper soaked in vinegar to relieve aching muscles.

Poultice made from a dirt-dauber's (wasp's) nest to remove carbuncle core.

Sassafras tea to thicken the blood.

Juice of a green walnut to treat ringworm.

Salve of kerosene and beef tallow to treat chapped hands.

Two tablespoons of India ink to eliminate tape worm.

Onions boiled in sulphur molasses for laxative.

Tea made from the scrapings of stallion hooves to cure the hives.

Warm brains of freshly killed rabbit applied to child's gums to relieve teething pains.

Hot blood of chicken to cure shingles.

Dr. William A. Hammond, whose early training as a military surgeon came at western frontier posts, was in his mid-thirties when he was named surgeon general of the army in 1861. Almost from the ground up, he built a huge medical organization for the Civil War—but dynamic activity creates antagonisms, and Doctor Hammond came into direct conflict with Secretary of War Edwin M Stanton, and he was dismissed after a bitter row in 1864. His famous "calomel order" of 1863 struck that drug and tartar emetic from army supply lists because he felt the military surgeons were over-using them to the detriment of the troops.

(Left) Among the earliest physicians in Seattle, Washington Territory, was Dr. H. B. Bagley. In 1881 he was the successful bidder to provide medical and surgical attendance for the patients at the King County "poor farm" and for prisoners in the county jail. His bid was $150 in scrip, payable quarterly. (Right) Dr. O. D. Cass came to Denver with the tide of gold-seekers and in 1860 was one of the physicians who attended the first meeting of the Jefferson Medical Society in a log cabin. The small gathering of doctors agreed on a national code of ethics for medicine and a uniform rate of $3 a visit.

A Gallery of Pioneers

DURING the 19th century in the sprawling territory west of the Mississippi River, thousands of doctors came and went through the years. Some made indelible impressions on the pages of history; others simply practiced their profession in relative obscurity and then faded from the scene with only a modest obituary.

It would be gross naivete to say there were no bad doctors, because the pages of the pioneer press prove that a few strayed from their oath of service. Most of them, though, were honorable, hard-working men with varying degrees of skill and ambition. Some were veritable "saints" in their communities, inspiring confidence and winning praise wherever their horse-and-buggy took them. For instance, there were men like Dr. Armistead H. Mitchell, who—according to the *New Northwest* of Deer Lodge, Montana, in 1882— "could go over this county and cure half the ailments with a pocketful of flour and a pint of aqua pura."

But good, bad or just average, the doctors of the Old West contributed immeasurably to the development of the frontier they helped roll back. Because there were so many, however, any attempt to include them all is an editorial impossibility. Many local favorites have had to be left out, not that they weren't deserving of mention, but somewhere an arbitrary line had to be drawn.

To those pioneer practitioners who have been thus overlooked, this symbolic gallery of old-timers is appropriately dedicated.

173

Dr. James Newton McCandless received his diploma from Jefferson Medical College in Philadelphia in 1863 and promptly marched off to war as a military surgeon. After Appomattox he went west, serving as a medical officer by contract at several posts, including Camp Lincoln and Fort Whipple in Arizona Territory. From 1868 until his death in 1904 he practiced in Prescott. He was, without question a true medical pioneer of the frontier.

Sharlot Hall Historical Museum of Arizona, Prescott

(Opposite page) Top row from left: Dr. John C. Davis, pioneer practitioner in Omaha, Nebraska; Dr. E. L. Smith, president of the Medical Society of Washington Territory, 1883-84; Dr. F. J. Bancroft, president of the Colorado Medical Society in 1881. Middle row: Dr. C. H. Merrick, superintendent of the King County (Washington Territory) "poor farm" in 1887; Dr. John F Morse, first editor of the California State Medical Journal; Dr. F. W. Hatch, president of the Sacramento Society for Medical Improvement, 1870. Bottom row: Dr. Simeon E. Josephi, first dean of the University of Oregon Medical School; Dr. Erasmus D. Leavitt, "gold rush" physician of Bannack, Montana; Dr. George W. Seifert, physician at Santa Clara College in 1884.

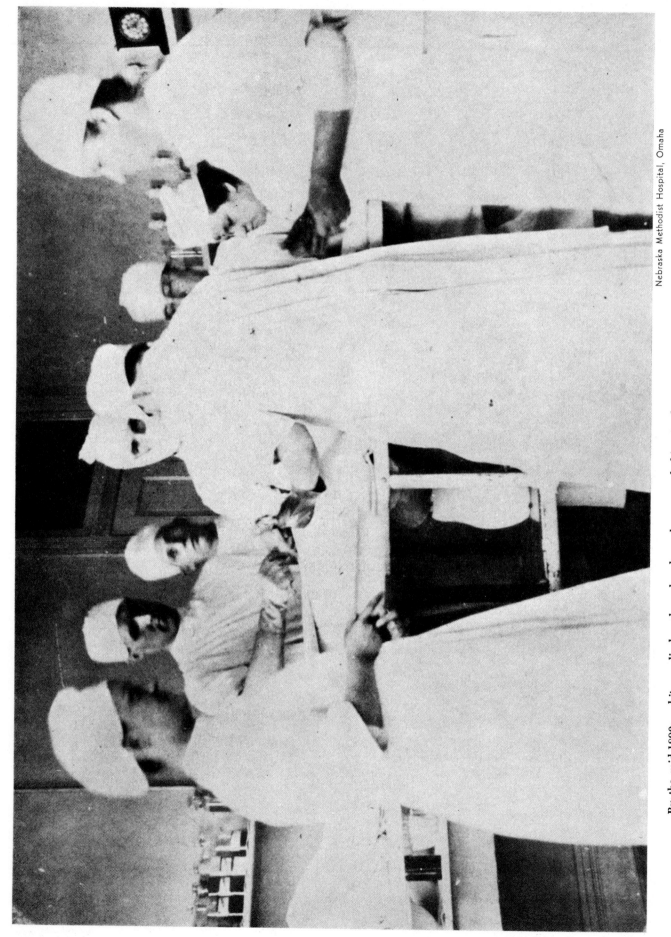

By the mid-1890s, white medical garb replaced regular street clothing in the surgeries of the West. Dr. William H. Stokes performed the operation shown above in the Nebraska Methodist Hospital in 1896. Note the clean-shaven faces of the male participants; this, too, was a major change. Surgical masks didn't come into general use until just before the turn of the century.

Wyoming State Archives and Historical Department

Dr. Fred Horton, a graduate of the Rush Medical School in Chicago, began practice in Newcastle, Wyoming Territory, in 1889. Like many country doctors, he was proud of the fact that he had delivered more than 2,000 healthy babies. Also, like numerous frontier physicians, he was active politically, holding county offices and serving as a state legislator.

State Historical Society of North Dakota

(Below left) Dr. Hugh Huger Toland was founder of the California medical school which bore his name and which later became the University of California's Department of Medicine in 1872. (Below right) Dr. Scott Helm, who served in 1897 as surgeon general of Arizona's territorial militia, was involved in a bitter court struggle when a fellow physician accused him of murder in an alleged abortion in 1891. Though Doctor Helm was acquitted, the scandal did little good for the medical profession. (At right) Doctor B. F. Slaughter of Bismarck, Dakota Territory, posed with his family in 1876.

(Top row) Dr. John LeConte, pioneer physician and teacher, was involved in the early history of the University of California; Dr. Charles Lewis Anderson arrived in Carson City, Nevada Territory, in 1862 and became noted as a botanist. Dr. O'Dillon B. Whitford was a gold-seeker and builder of hospitals in Montana. (Middle row) Gold eluded Dr. Luther J. Abbott in California, but he found a gratifying practice of four decades on the plains of Nebraska; Dr. Benjamin P. Magness was just 29 years old when he served in the Oklahoma territorial legislature. (Bottom row) In California, Dr. Thomas Muldrup Logan left the gold-field to battle the 1850 cholera epidemic in Sacramento; Dr. David Wall opened a drugstore in Vancouver, Washington Territory, in 1865 and practiced medicine there for 40 years; Dr. J. E. Summers, Sr., was a military surgeon whose stations included Fort Kearny, Nebraska.

Dr. Walter Reed, who won for himself an important niche in medical history because of his work in the fight against yellow fever, was first a military surgeon in the West. He saw service at Forts Omaha, Sidney and Robinson in Nebraska; Fort Keogh, Montana; Fort Snelling, Minnesota; Camp Apache, Fort Yuma and Fort Lowell in Arizona Territory. His studies of typhoid fever and malaria at the army posts in the Southwest raised questions in his mind which were to lead him to his successes against yellow jack.

The Nebraska Methodist Hospital and Deaconess Home in Omaha was one of many early-day institutions which struggled through a meager beginning to grow into a permanent, successful health center. Even in 1891 the hospital had a staff of neatly-clad nurses. There was little thought, however, of beautiful grounds, service efficiencies or even such vital factors as fire precaution. These were to come with the passage of time.

In 1887 the J. H. Harley Drugstore was admonishing residents of Lincoln, Nebraska, to drink Malto for the nerves with one window sign and a Sane's celery concoction with another. Celery tonics were particularly popular during that period; even the Sears, Roebuck catalog was offering its special Celery Malt Compound, "a recognized nerve and brain medicine."

Bibliography

ACKERKNECHT, ERWIN H., M.D. *A Short History of Medicine*. New York: The Ronald Press Company, 1955.

ASHBURN, P. M. *A History of the Medical Department of the United States Army*. Boston and New York: Houghton Mifflin Company, 1929.

BIGELOW, JOHN, ed. *Washington Hospitals: A Century of Service*. Seattle, Washington: Washington State Hospital Association, 1958.

BONNER, THOMAS N. *The Kansas Doctor*. Lawrence, Kansas: University of Kansas Press, 1959.

BROUGHER, JOHN C., M.D. "Early Medicine in the Pacific Northwest," *Northwest Medicine* (January, 1963).

———. "Pioneer Medicine in Clark County, Washington," *Northwest Medicine* (June, 1958).

CLAPESATTLE, HELEN. *The Doctors Mayo*. Garden City, New York: Garden City Publishing Co., Inc., 1941.

CLARK, HOWARD C., M.D. *A History of the Sedgwick County Medical Society*. (Kansas), undated.

CLINE, MERLE MAGNESS. "Dr. Benjamin Perry Magness, Pioneer Cowboy Doctor," *Prairie Lore*, The Southwestern Oklahoma Historical Society (October, 1966).

COOK, JAMES. *Remedies and Rackets*. New York: W. W. Norton & Company, Inc., 1958.

DANIELE, BETTIE MARIE and MCCONNELL, VIRGINIA. *The Springs of Manitou*. Denver, Colorado: Sage Books, 1964.

DICK, EVERETT, Ph.D. *The Sod-House Frontier 1854-1890*. New York and London: D. Appleton-Century Company, Inc., 1937.

DRURY, CLIFFORD MERRILL, Ph.D. *Marcus Whitman, M.D., Pioneer and Martyr*. Caldwell, Idaho: The Caxton Printers, Ltd., 1937.

DUNLOP, RICHARD. *Doctors of the American Frontier*. Garden City, New York: Doubleday & Company, Inc., 1965.

EASTMAN, CHARLES A., M.D. *From Deep Woods to Civilization*. Boston: Little, Brown & Co., 1920.

FEE, ART. "The Remarkable Dr. Keil," *Golden West Magazine* (November, 1966).

GIBSON, ARRELL M. "Medicine Show," *American West Magazine* (February, 1967).

GIBSON, JOHN M. *Physician to the World* (Gorgas). Durham, North Carolina: Duke University Press, 1950.

GRAY, GEORGE W. *The Advancing Front of Medicine*. New York and London: Whittlesey House, 1941.

GROH, GEORGE W. *Gold Fever*. New York: William Morrow & Company, Inc., 1966.

HAGGARD, HOWARD W., M.D. *Devils, Drugs, and Doctors*. New York: Blue Ribbon Books, Inc., 1929.

——. *The Doctor in History*. New Haven, Connecticut: Yale University Press, 1934.

——. *Mystery, Magic, and Medicine*. Garden City, New York: Doubleday, Doran & Company, Inc., 1933.

HARRIS, HENRY, M.D. *California's Medical Story*. San Francisco: J. W. Stacey, Inc., 1932.

HERTZLER, ARTHUR E., M.D. *The Horse and Buggy Doctor*. New York & London: Harper & Brothers, 1938.

HOLBROOK, STEWART H. *The Golden Age of Quackery*. New York: The Macmillan Company, 1959.

HOWE, F. S., M.D. *Deadwood Doctor*. Undated.

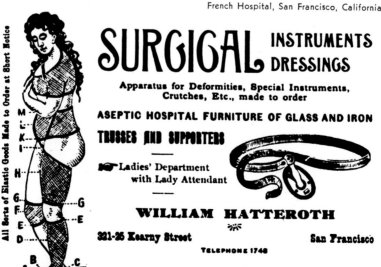

Pioneer drugstores everywhere looked and smelled much alike. With its marble-topped soda fountain and bottle-crammed shelves, this one in Lakota, North Dakota, was similar to a thousand others.

HRUBY, DANIEL D. *Mines to Medicine.* San Jose, California: O'Connor Hospital, 1965.

JONES, J. ROY, M.D. *History of the Medical Society of the State of California.* Sacramento, California: The Sacramento Society for Medical Improvement, 1964.

———. *Memories, Men and Medicine.* Sacramento, California: The Sacramento Society for Medical Improvement, 1950.

———. *Saddle Bags in Siskiyou.* Yreka, California: News-Journal Print Shop, 1953.

KIMBALL, MARIA B. *A Soldier Doctor of Our Army: James P. Kimball.* Boston and New York: Houghton Mifflin Co., 1917.

LARSELL, O. *The Doctor in Oregon:* Portland, Oregon: Binfords & Mort for the Oregon Historical Society, 1947.

LAUFE, ABE, ed. *An Army Doctor's Wife on the Frontier.* Pittsburgh: University of Pittsburgh Press, 1962.

LOVEJOY, ESTHER POHL, M.D. *Women Doctors of the World.* New York: The Macmillan Company, 1957.

LYMAN, GEORGE D. *John Marsh, Pioneer.* New York: Charles Scribner's Sons, 1930.

MASSENGILL, SAMUEL EVANS, M.D. *A Sketch of Medicine and Pharmacy.* Bristol, Tennessee: The S. E. Massengill Company, 1943.

McGILLICUDDY, JULIA B. *McGillicuddy: Agent.* Palo Alto, California: Stanford University Press, 1941.

MOORMAN, LEWIS J., M.D. *Pioneer Doctor.* Norman, Oklahoma: University of Oklahoma Press, 1951.

NEILSON, WILLIAM P., M.D., F.A.C.S. *The Doctor Was Here.* Guthrie, Oklahoma: Cooperative Publishing Company, undated.

NELSON, MARGARET A. *Home on the Range.* Boston: Chapman & Grimes, 1947.

OWENS-ADAIR, B.A., M.D. *Dr. Owens-Adair: Some of Her Life Experiences.* Portland, Oregon: Man & Beach, Printers, (undated).

PHILLIPS, PAUL C. *Medicine in the Making of Montana.* Missoula, Montana: The Montana Medical Association, 1962.

PREECE, HAROLD. *Living Pioneers.* Cleveland and New York: The World Publishing Company, 1952.

QUEBBEMAN, FRANCES E. *Medicine in Territorial Arizona.* Phoenix, Arizona: Arizona Historical Foundation, 1966.

REYNOLDS, HELEN BAKER. *Gold, Rawhide and Iron.* Palo Alto, California: Pacific Books, 1955.

ROBINSON, VICTOR, M.D. *The Story of Medicine.* New York: The New Home Library, 1943.

ROSENTHAL, ROBERT, M.D. "One Hundred Years of Organized Medicine in Minnesota," *Minnesota Medicine* (April, 1953).

SIGERIST, HENRY E., M.D. *American Medicine.* New York: W. W. Norton & Company, Inc., 1934.

SPRING, AGNES WRIGHT. "Dr. McGillicuddy's Diary," *Denver Brand Book* (Vol. IX, 1953).

TOLMIE, WILLIAM FRASER, M.D. *The Journals of William Fraser Tolmie, Physician and Fur Trader.* Vancouver, B.C.: Mitchell Press Limited, 1963.

TYLER, A. F. and AUERBACH, E. F. *History of Medicine in Nebraska.* Omaha, Nebraska: Magic City Printing Company, 1928.

WALTRIP, LELA and RUFUS. "Urling C. Coe—Adventures of a Range Doctor," *The West Magazine* (May, 1967).

WILSON, THELMA. "A Century of Medical Education in Oregon," *Northwest Medicine* (March, 1967).

The motor car signaled the end of the horse-and-buggy era. Doctor Rininger (with derby) had the third auto in Seattle, Washington, and all over the West, other physicians were shifting to a new mode of transportation—just as they were shifting to new techniques and medical philosophies in their profession.

Index

Though the horse-and-buggy doctor was to fade from the scene, he left a reputation for diligence and perseverance which grows even greater with the passage of time. Dr. W. O. Bridges of Omaha, Nebraska, was typical of hundreds of pioneer practitioners who traveled endless miles in spindly vehicles to visit their patients.

Northwest Medicine

187

Nebraska Methodist Hospital, Omaha

Dr. Harold Gifford, Sr., was one of Nebraska's pioneer ophthalmologists in an era when specialization was just becoming a factor in the practice of medicine.

189

Toland, Dr. Hugh H., 59, 177.
Toland Medical College (San Francisco, California), 59, 62, 160, 177.
Tolmie, Dr. William Fraser, 21-22, 24.
Tomahas, 25.
Tombstone, Arizona, 77.
Tooele County, Utah, 161.
Topeka, Kansas, 57, 66, 108.
Transylvania University Medical School, 57.
Treaty of Guadalupe Hidalgo, 32.
Trierweiler, Dr. J. E., 5.
Trinidad, Colorado, 69, 111, 129.
Tucson, Arizona, 77, 85, 123, 136.
Tuttle, Bishop Daniel S., 114.

U

Underground Railway, 106.
Union College, 100.
Union Pacific Coal Company, 163.
Union Pacific Museum, 109.
Union Pacific Railroad, 122.
University of Barcelona, 21.
University of California Medical School, 59, 62, 160, 177-178.
University of Denver, 107.
University of Dublin, 23.
University of Glasgow, 21.
University of Michigan Medical School, 160.
University of Oregon Medical School, 62, 115, 121, 175.
University of Padua, 26.
University of Pennsylvania Medical School, 25, 57, 90, 144.
University of the Pacific Medical Department, 61.
U. S. *Pharmacopeia*, 14.
U. S. Weather Bureau, 37, 39.
Utah Hot Springs, 127.

V

Vancouver, Capt. George, 24.
Vancouver Island, 24.
Vancouver Ladies of Charity, 116.
Vancouver, Washington, 116, 127, 178.
Veatch, Dr. John A., 102.
Victoria, British Columbia, 24.
Virginia City, Montana, 49, 75, 101, 124.

W

Waiilatpu Mission, 25, 114.
Wall, Dr. David, 178.
Walla Walla, Washington, 25, 33, 97, 99.
Walters, Dr. J. W., 100.
Walthill, Nebraska, 118.
Wanzer, Dr. Lucy M. Field, 160.
Warren, Francis E., 108-109.
Washburn College School of Medicine, 57.
Washington County, Oregon, 105.
Washington, D.C., 25.

Equitable of Iowa

"For these friends of ours who have gone before there is now no more toil . . . they ride no longer the lonely roads that knew them so well. . . ."

OLIVER WENDELL HOLMES, M.D.

Washington, George, 56.
Washington-on-the-Brazos, Texas, 23.
Wassaja (see Montezuma, Dr. Carlos), 16-17.
Wayside Mission Hospital (Seattle, Washington), 118-119, 124-125.
Weed, Dr. Gideon A., 104, 109.
Weiser, Dr. Josiah S., 29-30.
Wells-Fargo, 83.
West Beaver Creek (Kansas), 102, 104.
Wheeler, Gen. Joseph, 35.
White, Dr. Elijah, 25.
Whitford, Dr. O'Dillon B., 178.
Whitman, Dr. Marcus, 25, 114.
Whitman, Narcissa, 25.
Wichita, Kansas, 11, 52, 65, 85, 88, 117, 135.
Wichita (Kans.) *Eagle*, 65.
Wichita (Kans.) Hospital, 11.
Wichita (Kans.) Training School for Nurses, 166.
Willamette University Medical Department, 60, 62-63, 160.
Williams, Dr. J. W., 27.
William N. Byers & Co., 100.
Winslow House (Minneapolis, Minnesota), 124.

Winton Runabout auto, 94.
Women's Medical College of Pennsylvania, 157.
Wood, Dr. Leonard, 35, 38, 104.
Woodhouse, Dr. Samuel W., 33.
Wood, Josephine Catherine Chatterly, 160.
World War I, 94, 164.
Wounded Knee Creek (massacre), 17, 36, 43.
Wyeth, Dr. Jacob, 26.
Wyeth, Nathaniel, 26.

X

X-ray, 70-71, 77-78, 90, 94.

Y

Yankton, South Dakota, 5, 55, 102, 105, 107, 132, 161, 166.
Yellowstone National Park, 19, 25, 97.
Yreka, California, 83, 116.
Yreka (Calif.) *Journal*, 66.
Yuba River, 100.

Z

Zervan, Dr. Frederico, 24, 114.
Zillah, Washington, 94.

Neal E. Miller Collection